JOHN PAUL II,
MAN OF PRAYER

John Paul II, Man of Prayer
The Spiritual Life of a Saint

CLARE ANDERSON

&

JOANNA BOGLE

GRACEWING

First published in 2014 by
Gracewing
2 Southern Avenue
Leominster
Herefordshire HR6 0QF
United Kingdom
www.gracewing.co.uk

The rights of Clare Anderson and Joanna Bogle
to be identified as the author of this work have been asserted in
accordance with the Copyright, Designs and Patents Act 1988.

© 2014 Clare Anderson and Joanna Bogle

ISBN 978 085244 832 8

Typeset by Gracewing

Cover design by Bernardita Peña Hurtado

Dedicated to our husbands

Laurence Anderson and Jamie Bogle

with love and thanks

"Do not be afraid!"

Pope John Paul II

"Perfect love casts out fear … and he who fears is not perfected in love."

1 John 4:18

CONTENTS

FOREWORD

HEN POPE JOHN PAUL II was asked, 'How does the Pope pray?' he replied, 'You would have to ask the Holy Spirit!' Then he spoke of 'the missionary dimension of prayer and the Pope' as 'Prayer is a search for God, but also a revelation of God.' He said: 'Because the Pope is a witness of Christ and a minister of the Good News, he is a man of joy and a man of hope, a man of fundamental affirmation of the value of existence, the value of creation and a hope in the future life.' (*Crossing The Threshold of Hope*, 1994)

In this fascinating book, the prayerful and spiritual rock-bed of the successor of St Peter is drawn out. Pope John Paul II's whole life and witness could be said to be like that of Christ—often in the Garden of Gethsemane but translucent with the hope of the Resurrection.

In the midst of suffering and seeming hopelessness, both personally and as Pope, Karol Josef Wojtyła turned again and again to Christ's comforting, and yet challenging, words: 'Do not be afraid' and he would add, as in his inaugural homily, 'Open the doors to Christ.' This conviction and faith was also there in his motto: *Totus Tuus* ('All for you', or 'Totally yours') as he stood with Our Lady at the foot of the Cross, suffering with Christ and with humanity.

This witness of faith was made apparent to me when, with pilgrims from *Aid to the Church in Need* in the great Jubilee Year, I stood by the Colosseum on 7

May 2000. Large cauldron lamps were lit in front of Rome's ancient Colosseum at the Ecumenical Commemoration of Witnesses to the Faith in the twentieth Century. As I watched Pope John Paul II, head bent in prayer on a grey and damp evening, the light from those lamp stands glowed stronger. The historical joining of the early Church witness and that of recent martyrs was a dramatic, powerful and unifying Petrine statement, focusing on the suffering of Christ in His Body the Church.

Like a light out of darkness, the witness of faith of those who suffered oppression and persecution in communist times, was a surprise to many. So also with Pope John Paul II: the Polish priest, bishop and cardinal became a light for all people.

I had the privilege to meet Pope John Paul II, who was deeply grateful for the support *Aid to the Church in Need* gave to the suffering Church in Eastern Europe. In Poland, *Aid to the Church in Need* helped fund the building by volunteers of the Church of Our Lady of Poland (or Arka Pana—Lord's Ark) in Nowa Huta, completed in 1977 after communist authorities had stubbornly refused permission for twenty years.

Many years later, on 27 June 2001, Pope John Paul once again met the founder of *Aid to the Church in Need*, Fr Werenfried van Straaten, at a ceremony in Lviv, Ukraine. The foundation stone of a new seminary and theological academy was being blessed. That day, with Pope John Paul in his white papal cassock and Fr Werenfried in his white Norbertine habit, it seemed as though the two figures dressed in white had come to announce the Resurrection—like the angels at the tomb of Christ. Speaking at the ceremony, Pope John Paul reflected on the years of suffering and martyrdom, but also on the hundreds of new vocations when he said:

> In their resistance to the mystery of evil, the strength of faith and of the grace of Christ was able to shine brightly, despite human weakness. Their indomitable witness has shown itself to be the seed of new Christians ... If God blesses your land with many vocations and if the seminaries are full—and this is a source of hope for your Church—this is surely one of the fruits of their sacrifice.

The 'fruits of their sacrifice', of witness through suffering—that surely was the final witness of Pope John Paul II. It came from a life of deep prayer, commitment and trust in the triumph of Christ crucified and risen for each and every one of us. There will be many different reflections on the life of Karol Josef Wojtyła, perhaps many with the benefit or arrogance of hindsight. Yet, the heart of Pope John Paul II was immersed in God's love, as shown, lived and witnessed to us on the cross. Paradoxically, the light of Christ often shines brightest in the darkness of suffering and in this 'man from the East' the star shone brightest in his witness in the months before his death.

Neville Kyrke-Smith
National Director
Aid to the Church in Need UK

INTRODUCTION

PERSON'S INTERIOR LIFE can only really be known by that person, but in this book we seek to discover the spiritual message of the life of Karol Wojtyła, John Paul II. We attempt this by exploring three aspects: his words, spoken and written, his deeds, and the accounts of others.

Karol Wojtyła was a very private person and he rarely spoke of his interior life. Rooted in Poland, he was heavily influenced by Spanish mysticism. This is a not a man easily categorised.

John Paul was *Time* magazine's 'Man of the Century', but he himself said that he could only be known 'from the inside'. So we dare to share something of a spiritual journey with him.

Prayer is not separate from the rest of life. A book on John Paul II's spiritual life will inevitably mean exploring other aspects: his understanding of freedom, his message on human love, his relationship with his native country.

In a sense, the great Christian mystics of history are alike: their faith is utterly direct and simple. Wojtyła was a complex individual—an intellectual giant, a philosopher of brilliance, a widely read academic—and we will never know the struggles he had in co-operating with God's grace. His faith consisted primarily in a thirst for God, in the knowledge that only in God can man's desires be fulfilled, and not in material things or in ideologies.

Those who truly seek Christ are at heart profoundly simple: they want to know God personally, in a love-relationship, not merely to know 'about' God in the manner of the learned. We can see this too in Pope Benedict XVI, one of the greatest theologians of the twentieth century, and a close colleague of John Paul II. His faith was described as 'like that of a young child on the day of his first Communion'.

John Paul's exhortation 'Do not be afraid!' with which he opened his pontificate alluded to this simple self-giving to God. Christ was at the centre of John Paul's being. He was able to inspire and uplift people on an extraordinary scale, because his life was given over to God and lived with daily faith and courage.

Investigating someone's prayer-life can seem rather intrusive. But John Paul has challenged us, while working on this book, to get to know Christ better, and to understand the true nature of a life lived in union with God. Studying the inner life of this most remark-able man—philosopher, poet, playwright, priest, Pope—we came to understand that at the heart was a simplicity and joy. He has been called 'John Paul the Great' and certainly his pontificate was a remarkable one—the collapse of Communism as a power-block, the introduction of World Youth Days, the teaching on the Theology of the Body, the missionary journeys to country after country. He has now been declared a saint, and joins the ranks of those canonised by the Church: in exploring his spiritual life, we can learn what inspired and nourished this great man.

Acknowledgements

WE ARE INDEBTED to His Eminence Cardinal Stanisław Dziwisz, Archbishop of Krakow, for so generously giving us his time and talking to us with such friendliness and warmth.

Warmest thanks, too to Father Jan Machniak for his help, advice, and translations—and for showing us around the Archbishop's Palace and explaining the history and significance of the various rooms.

Grateful thanks to Jan Kruszewska for her translation of Polish reminiscences and to Maria Renek for introducing us to Kalwaria.

Special thanks to Dennis O'Keeffe for the background information on Poland in the 1980s, to Pawel Kloczowski for giving us so much help, making us so welcome in Krakow, and sharing memories of Archbishop Wojtyła, and to Miłowit Kuninski for much useful background information.

And our huge appreciative thanks to Iwo Bender and Tadeusz Smiarowski, EWTN's Polish team, for the unforgettable days in Krakow, Wadowice and Częstochowa.

Clare Anderson
Joanna Bogle

1

THE EARLY YEARS

IT IS IMPOSSIBLE to enter the parish church of Wadowice without being reminded of the town's most famous son. The entire ceiling of the baroque building is covered with scenes depicting each one of Pope John Paul II's fourteen encyclicals. There is a side chapel with a large statue of the former pope and a white papal skull cap and rosary.

It was in this place that Karol Josef Wojtyła was baptised on 20 June 1920 at the age of one month. Father Franciszek Zak, the officiating priest, was a military chaplain, appropriately enough as the baby's father was an army officer. Situated at a major cross-roads linking Poland to Vienna, the county town of Wadowice had a vibrant cultural and social mix and excellent schools. Catholic Christianity predominated, but there were good relations with the local Jewish community where the young Karol would feel especially welcome. This cosmopolitan atmosphere would instil a cheerful outward-looking optimism into the young Wojtyła's sense of Polish nationhood.

Karol Senior and Emilia Kaczorowska reputedly met at church in Krakow and it is said that Emilia, the mother of the future pope, wanted two sons, a doctor and a priest. A daughter, Olga, died in infancy. Young Karol was her third and last child. Born in the month of May, Our Lady's month, it is said that the first sounds the new baby heard was a hymn to Our Lady being sung in the church next door.

The Pope was later to write that his mother's influence on him 'must have been great' but he seems to have had few memories of her. Never robust, Emilia became increasingly frail after Karol's birth—doctors had advised her to end the pregnancy rather than risk childbirth[1]—and in 1929, a little before Karol's ninth birthday, she died of heart disease. Emilia's death brought father and son even closer. With Karol's elder brother Edmund studying medicine in Krakow, there were just the two of them at home. Karol Senior was bereft at losing his wife and devoted himself increasingly to prayer. His youngest son, nicknamed Lolek, perhaps detecting a great sadness in his father, spent as much of his free time as possible with him. Friends who wished to spend time with Karol had to visit the Wojtyła apartment. Karol Jr's best friend, Jerzy Kluger, remembered catching sight of 'The Captain', as he was called, in the next room kneeling in silent prayer before an image of Our Lady of Częstochowa.

His father was the first major influence on the future pope's spirituality, his military background perhaps providing an early grounding in discipline that was at the heart of Pope John Paul's spiritual life. Born in Bielsko Biała, a village about 18 miles from Wadowice, the older Karol Wojtyła was a tailor's son who initially followed in his father's footsteps before joining the Austro-Hungarian (and later the Polish) army, finally resigning in 1927, for health reasons. Largely self-taught, he was an avid reader with an especial love of Polish history and literature. The little library of books in the modest apartment had a 'little bit of everything' according to Kluger. Lolek and his friends would love to listen to tales of old battles and Polish heroism. The captain portrayed the stories as a kind of drama, evoking the sights and sounds of battle, holding his young audience spellbound. It is perhaps through his father's tales that Lolek's love of drama and the spoken word took root. He presumably also inherited his acting talent from his father.

Although heartbroken at the death of his wife, the Captain devoted himself to providing a happy home for his family. In 1932, however, tragedy struck again when Edmund, their beloved Mundek, died of scarlet fever at the age of twenty-six. It was Mundek who had encouraged Lolek to play football. We know that the future pope had a life-long love of hiking, skiing and the outdoor life, but he seems to have been less good at competitive sports. In his book about his friendship with the Pope, Jerzy Kluger writes of beating him at tennis and ping pong, and even that Lolek was a bit clumsy on his feet. If so, then one can recognise the care of an older brother in encouraging a field sport to develop speed and co-ordination. A photograph of Edmund shows a handsome young man, similar to his younger brother in looks and presumably not unlike him in other ways. He took his medical calling seriously, going out of his way to care for the most gravely ill, which made him immensely popular. This devotion to duty was to cost him his life—he had volunteered to care for a contagious young patient, dying in isolation in hospital, and paid the price with his own life. It is tempting to see the example of compassion and selfless duty in the older brother as a profound influence on the future pope's spiritual and moral development. Also, by the age of twelve, Karol Wojtyła had learned the difficult lesson of accepting God's will in all things. At the time of his mother's death, a neighbour expressed sympathy with the young Lolek who simply replied 'It is the will of God'.

If Lolek's early years were troubled by loss, it is clear that his strength initially came from being a greatly-loved child. A portrait photograph taken of Emilia with Karol as a chubby infant shows a contented soul, the eyes radiating joy and pride in her youngest child. After her death, the Captain became increasingly protective of his children, notably his youngest. He cooked meals and repaired clothes, leaving his gifted son to concentrate on his schoolwork. When Jerzy Kluger's grandmother asked Karol Senior if she might give his son a small motorbike for his birthday, he pleaded with her not to, fearing for his son's safety. When Lolek cut his head while playing, the Kluger women tended the injury before the Captain could see it.[2]

The Wojtyłas were not wealthy, but by the standards of the time they were certainly not poor. The small apartment was rented but there was always enough food. There was never any desire to acquire material goods or wealth for its own sake. They were a people whose faith went beyond Sunday observance to encompass all of life. The Captain may have seemed a trifle austere to outsiders, but for him what mattered was a person's character, not their wealth or social standing. Nor did the deep closeness that the family felt for each other exclude the wider community, which included the Jewish townspeople.

Jerzy Kluger's father was the head of Wadowice's Jewish community. Wealthy and accomplished (he was a fine violinist), he had a high opinion of the Captain and when a celebrated Jewish singer was due to perform in the town synagogue, the Captain and his son were among the guests. On another occasion, when Jerzy Kluger sought his friend in the local church, a woman made it clear that he was unwelcome there. Young Karol, however, thought otherwise and said 'Doesn't she know that we are all children of God?'

When the shadow of Nazism threatened the town's Jews, a young neighbour called to visit the Wojtyłas to tell them of her decision to emigrate. The captain embraced her and begged her not to believe that all Polish Catholics were hostile to Jews. This attitude, sadly not universal in pre-war Poland (or Europe) gives us an indication of the values which the young Karol was learning from his father and which would remain with him throughout his life. He would not speak of Jews as 'other' but 'our elder brothers and sisters'. It would be Pope John Paul II who would make the unprecedented decision to have formal diplomatic ties with Israel.

Karol Sr was respected in the town as a man of integrity and honour, and he impressed on his sons the need to live justly in dealings with others. Pope John Paul II wrote that their home together was a kind of 'domestic seminary' in which his father taught principally by example. Their day had an almost monastic structure, beginning usually with Mass before Lolek went to school. After lunch, which was usually taken in a local restaurant, would follow a couple of hours recreation, then homework. Prayer was a constant in their lives; the Captain prayed often during the day, on his knees. The two read the Bible and said the rosary together. Sometimes the young boy would wake in the night and see his father kneeling in the dark, praying silently.[3]

It is sometimes said that our early image of God is dependent on the kind of father we have had—in the young Karol Wojtyła's case, he grew up with a loving

and protective father who passed on his faith by
example and not fear. Undemonstrative by nature, the
military man reflected a faith that was natural and
manly; something that a sensitive and intelligent boy
would be glad, not embarrassed, to emulate. One
evening when Lolek expressed worry about a maths
exam the next day, his father gave him the prayer to
the Holy Spirit, and advised him to pray it daily, which
he did from then on. Speaking in 1979 to a conference
of Catholic Charismatics, he said

> When I was in school, at the age of twelve or
> thirteen ... My father gave me a book on prayer.
> He opened it to a page and said to me 'Here you
> have the prayer to the Holy Spirit. You must
> say this prayer every day of your life.' I have
> remained obedient to this order that my father
> gave nearly fifty years ago... This was my first
> spiritual initiation, so I can understand all the
> different charisms. All of them are part of the
> riches of the Lord.[4]

Clearly, he never forgot a spiritual lesson.

Wadowice's parish church was next door to the
apartment block where the Wojtyłas lived, it took
almost no time to nip across for daily Mass. The small
apartment looked out over the side of the church, in
which was set a sundial. This bore the inscription
Tempus fugit, aeternitas manet—time flies, eternity
remains. This sobering thought wove its way, con-
sciously and unconsciously, throughout Karol's life,
as we shall see. He was never a person to waste time.

The young Karol became an altar boy and it was
through the church that he met the second person to
influence his spiritual development. When Karol was
ten, Fr Kazimierz Figlewicz came to Wadowice to teach

catechism in the school. He soon became his confessor and spiritual advisor. When Fr Figlewicz was transferred to the cathedral in Krakow, he maintained contact with the devout young schoolboy and invited him to attend Holy Week services at the cathedral. These were to affect the young boy profoundly and leave lasting memories. It was probably Fr Figlewicz who planted the seed of the future pope's vocation.

In a country where culture and religion merged, reminders of the faith were everywhere. The year was marked by feasts and seasons; sharing the *oplatek* bread at Christmas (a tradition that the Holy Father maintained even in the Vatican) brought all the family together, as did the pilgrimages that were regularly undertaken by most people.

Close to Wadowice is one of Poland's most best-loved pilgrimage centres, Kalwaria Zebrzydowska. Dating from the 1600s, it is hardly known outside Poland but remains deeply ingrained in the devotion and practice of the Polish people. A wooded hillside was landscaped to resemble the original scene outside Jerusalem and forty baroque chapels built at intervals to commemorate the way of the Cross and the life of the Virgin Mary. There is a monastery complex whose church houses a famous icon of the Mother of God. Every year thousands of Poles make the pilgrimage, walking from chapel to chapel, meditating on Christ's passion or the sorrows of his mother. The Kalwaria is the second most visited shrine after Częstochowa.

It is not difficult to imagine the young Lolek travelling to this place on foot with his father and brother, or being carried as a very young child on his brother's shoulders. At Easter there would be mystery plays which may well have appealed to the future actor and dramatist. It was to the Kalwaria that the Captain brought his young son after the death of his mother, to pray for her soul and find comfort in the cross, as so many others have done throughout its history. Polish Catholicism is rich in symbolism and at the same time strongly evokes the independent spirit of the people. Poland in early spring can be bitterly cold and snow is not unusual, yet huge crowds still converge on the Kalwaria in Lent. The climate and terrain contribute in no small measure to the sturdiness and resilience of its people. Accustomed to hardship and strong in faith, the Polish people would nourish a strong sense of courage and steadfastness that would serve them well during the upheavals and terrible sufferings of the twentieth century.

It would have been too far to travel regularly to the monastery of Jasna Gora in Częstochowa, the home of the Black Madonna icon, as it is more than 80 miles from Wadowice. A copy of this image hung in almost all Polish homes, and as noted earlier, it was often under this icon that the Captain would kneel at prayer. There is a legend that it was painted by St Luke, but its history is obscure until it arrived in Poland about six hundred years ago. Since then, no other image so encapsulates the soul of Poland than the Black Madonna, perhaps because it has known more than its fair share of violence. On the cheek of the Virgin Mary are two slash marks, said to have been delivered in 1430 by a Swedish Hussite soldier. Poles believe that this image has saved them on numerous occasions. As a student, Karol Wojtyła visited the shrine, and returned shortly after becoming Pope. He kept an image of the Black Madonna in the Vatican, which remains to this day.

If this region of Poland is rich in shrines, it also does not lack saints. Wadowice itself can boast St Raphael Kalinowski, a Carmelite friar who died in Wadowice in 1907 at the age of seventy-two. Born in 1835 in Vilnius, then under Russian control, his family were Polish aristocrats who prayed earnestly for union between Rome and the Eastern Orthodox churches. A brilliant student, young Kalinowski studied engineering in St Petersburg and was appointed a military engineer in the Russian army. With the Polish uprising of 1863, he resigned his commission and joined the rebels, although he knew that the revolt was doomed. Sentenced to death by the Russians but eventually deported to Siberia, Kalinowski became widely respected by Poles, Lithuanians and Russians alike for the holiness of his life and especially his care for others. On his return to Poland, he worked briefly as a tutor to a prince, but eventually joined the Carmelites at the age of forty-two taking the name of Raphael. Having lived so long as a layman, St Raphael was convinced that everyone is called to be holy, an insight that would later be promulgated by the Second Vatican Council. He wrote a biography of his friend Hermann Cohen, the Jewish pianist who became a Carmelite priest. He prayed tirelessly for the conversion of Russia. It's not known how much his life influenced the young Wojtyła but the future pope would certainly have heard about him. One saying of his would have struck a chord with Pope John Paul:

> If I give myself in the service of others, it means that the others have the right to take anything that belongs to me. I allow them to do it, as Christ did ... and it does not mean only material goods, but also my time and my spiritual goods.

St Raphael was beatified and canonised by Pope John Paul II.

Another saint canonised by Pope John Paul and a near contemporary of Kalinowski was Albert Chmielowski. Born of aristocratic parents in 1845 on the outskirts of Krakow, Adam Chmielowski was expected to inherit the family estate and initially studied agriculture. Becoming more interested in politics he supported the Polish uprising of 1863 in which he lost a leg. Fearing for his life, he fled Poland and made his home in Ghent, Belgium, where he discovered a talent for painting. Returning to Krakow in 1874, he became a well-known artist. But Adam's political convictions grew as he noticed the suffering of the city's poor. His work among the homeless inspired much of his best art, but eventually he decided to give up painting to live among the poor as one of them. Like St Raphael, he was unattached to any religious order for the first forty-two years of his life, but in 1887 he joined the Third Order of St Francis, calling himself Brother Albert. The following year he founded a new Franciscan order dedicated to serving the poor. He died in 1916.

Because of the tension between his life as an artist and his growing concern to be of service to others, Brother Albert had a profound effect on the future pope. The young Karol Wojtyła had planned to be an actor and was also an accomplished poet and playwright. As a young priest he wrote a play about Brother Albert called *Our God's Brother*. Later, as Pope, he would write that Brother Albert played a part in his formation 'because I found in him a real spiritual support and example in leaving behind the world of art, literature and the theatre, and in making the radical choice of a vocation to the Priesthood'.[5]

Spiritual formation does not take place in isolation; people, events, the surrounding culture, help to make us what we are. Much has been made of Wojtyła's Polishness and his devoutly Catholic family; of course these contributed to his development, but they do not explain everything about him. Christianity is not a set of propositions or a tradition to be handed on within a culture, but a faith in a person who Christians believe came to earth to die for us; such an act demands a personal response.

In an interview with a French journalist, the Holy Father said:

> From my earliest years I found myself in an atmosphere of faith and in a social milieu deeply rooted in the presence and action of the Church. In spite of this—perhaps because of this—it seems to me all the more important to assert that faith 'as personal response to the word of God, expressed in Jesus Christ' is created and develops ceaselessly ... At the same time I am convinced that never at any period of my life was my faith a purely 'sociological' phenomenon resulting from the habits or customs of my environment, in a word, from the fact that others around me 'believed and acted like that'... when I look objectively at my own faith I have always observed that it has had nothing to do with any kind of conformism, that it was born in the depths of my own 'self' and that it was also the fruit of my intellectual search for an answer to the mysteries of man and of the world.[6]

Notes

1   See M. Kindziuk, *Matka Papieza* (Warsaw: Znak, 2013). Reported in *Lifenews* (16 October 2013).

2   This and other anecdotes from John Paul's childhood are recounted in J. Kluger, *The Pope and I* (New York: Orbis Books 2010).

3   See G.Weigel, *Witness to Hope* (London: HarperCollins, 1999), pp. 30–31.

4   John Paul II, *Address to Charismatic Renewal Movement* (11 December 1979).

5   John Paul II, *Gift and Mystery* (New York: Image/Doubleday, 1996), p. 33.

6   A. Frossard, *Be Not Afraid! André Frossard in Conversation with John Paul II* (London: Bodley Head, 1984).

2

'IT'S NOT DIFFICULT TO BE A SAINT!'

AROL WOJTYŁA BEGAN studying at the Jagiellonian University in 1938, fully intending to
become an actor. Moving to Krakow, father
and son found an apartment in the Dębniki area in the
south west of the city. It was a short walk from the
university but unfortunately the conditions were poor.
It was a basement, poorly-lit and damp. Lolek's new
friends called it 'the catacombs'. It was part of a
building belonging to relatives of Lolek's mother.

Young Karol threw himself into his studies — he was
fascinated by philology and the history and development of language. He came to see how the faculty of
language makes culture possible, especially theatre,
poetry and literature. He had been acting since he was
eight; Wadowice had a gifted theatrical family, the
Kotlarczyks; the most brilliant of them, Mieczyslaw,
would eventually move to Krakow at Karol's invitation and start the Rhapsodic Theatre in secret. When
Germany invaded Poland in 1939 theatres were
banned, along with all public entertainment other than
the bland, the banal and propaganda.[1] No one was
fooled; among Poles the phrase went 'only pigs go to
the cinema'. All intellectual life went underground.
The Jagiellonian University was closed, and young
Karol found work first in a quarry and then in a
chemical plant. Overworked and poorly paid, he lost
weight; any extra food went to his father whose health

was failing due to poor nourishment and the damp and cold of their apartment.

The Rhapsodic Theatre was based on Kotlarczyk's central message, that of the 'Theatre of the Living Word'. It was the word itself that mattered. This emulated the style of drama that had traditionally been played in the houses of the Polish aristocracy in the days when Poland did not officially exist on any map but Polish culture and language was kept alive in this way. Set, costume and makeup were minimal, the script everything. Lines were declaimed slowly and carefully in a way that emphasised every aspect of meaning—'acting' with vivid gestures, expressions and emphasis was avoided. The plays or epic poems were intended as vehicles for teaching morality or an ideal. Narrative, plot, all attempts at everyday realism, were subordinate to the deeper meaning. This is the very opposite of art as entertainment. Under Nazi rule such theatre was obviously a grave threat, putting as it did the need for the audience to discern the message and apply it as they will. Totalitarianism, whether Nazi or Communist, fears human choice so people have to be told what to think. Those who performed and those who attended any kind of Polish theatre in Nazi-run Poland risked death. Kotlarczyk's brainchild was ideal for underground theatre as no props were needed— there was no need for anything but the players them- selves. The Rhapsodic Theatre performed clandes- tinely over a hundred times during the German occupation (not counting rehearsals). It was popular as people wanted to hear Polish spoken, especially in the words of their greatest writers, to be reminded of their national history and identity as Poles.

In a letter to Kotlarczyk, the young Wojtyła wrote that he wanted to create 'a theatre that will be a church where the national spirit will burn'. He felt more and more that theatre, particularly this kind of subtle, thought-provoking drama, would be his path in life. In a world where people were not free to express their opinions, an inner freedom must be cultivated. This idea would remain with Karol for the rest of his life.

It was at this time, when he was heavily involved with acting, that young Karol met the man who was to change forever his relationship with God. If Karol's father taught him what it is to be a Christian man, and Fr Figlewicz what it is to be a priest, Karol would now find a way to satisfy his growing spiritual hunger.

Nearby Stanislaus Kostka church was run by the Salesians, of whom later the Pope was to say 'I believe the presence of the Salesians played an important role in the formation of my vocation'.[2] John Paul II was characteristically reticent in saying how, but it is not difficult to detect in the sons of John Bosco a similar focus to his own. Formed in 1859 by a dynamic Turin priest as an outreach to street children, the Salesians founded schools and became great educators. The Order did much good among the very poor, to teach them the faith and lift them by education out of poverty and exploitation. As pastor, teacher and Pope, Wojtyła in his ministry always harboured a particular concern for the young. The Salesians, however, are an active order, and Karol's spiritual path was to take a very different turn.

Jan Leopold Tyranowski was born in 1900, the son of a tailor. Thoughtful and intelligent, Jan worked as an accountant but following a conversion experience he reverted to tailoring, working from home which allowed him the time and privacy to concentrate on his prayer life. Before the war, he had been involved in Catholic Action but a phrase he had heard in a sermon, 'it's not difficult to be a saint' affected him deeply. This was at a time when holiness was associated more with nuns and priests than laypeople and lay spirituality was more action-oriented. He lived with his mother who must presumably have given him the space to follow the life that he had chosen.

From all accounts, St Stanislaus Kostka parish was a dynamic one, with a significant number of young people—it probably had a rather 'studenty' atmosphere due to its location. After a retreat and Bible discussion group in 1940, the parish priest asked Tyranowski to organise a Living Rosary group among the young people. Up to the war, there had been several priests in the parish, but all except two had been deported to Dachau and now it was impossible for the priests to do everything unaided.

The Living Rosary movement had been founded in 1826 in France by Pauline Marie Jaricot (1700–1862). The fifteen decades of the rosary were divided among fifteen members, each of whom pledged to recite a decade and undertake spiritual reading. The aim was to pray for the preservation of the Faith in Catholic countries and the conversion of sinners. It is likely that, in 1940, the preservation of Poland itself, the strengthening of all Catholics and the conversion of the invading forces were high in the group's intentions. As such meetings were banned, membership of the Living Rosary could incur a death sentence.

Tyranowski set to work recruiting young people for the rosary group. He would wait by the church door after Mass until he saw anyone he thought would be suitable and then approach them with an invitation to join. He had met Karol Wojtyła at the Scripture study group, and knew him to be exactly the kind of person he needed. Lolek's first impression of the shy middle-aged man had not been especially favourable. Tyranowski had an old-fashioned manner; he was slim, fair with delicate features and a rather high voice. He seemed very intense—so much so that at least one other member of the group originally thought he was a member of the secret police. Some thought him a bit mad and there were rumours that Tyranowski had received psychiatric treatment in the past. He was certainly well-read in the emerging theories of human personality and would have found this knowledge useful when it came to advising group members about spiritual reading and practice.

The Living Rosary met in church to recite the rosary together; from all accounts it was a rather rote, dull affair. Perhaps this was done in order not to alarm the authorities who had spies everywhere. The real business of the group went on in Tyranowski's flat in Rozana Street, a short distance from the church and the Wojtyła apartment. It was here that Tyranowski made himself available at any time to members serious about developing their spiritual life.

'All his efforts, instructions, advice and methods of teaching were designed to show us how to remain in the presence of God in prayer and in daily life' wrote Fr Miecyzsław Malinski, another member. Malinski was a year younger than Lolek, the two met through the rosary group and became friends. When Malinski remarked privately that he found Tyranowski a bit odd, Lolek replied 'I found him the most normal person in the world.'[3]

Despite his old-fashioned air, Tyranowski used his knowledge of psychology to good effect, applying it with his gift of discernment to advise each person who came to him. 'Anyone can be a saint!' he exhorted his hearers who were as astonished as he had been by these words. Saints traditionally lived in monasteries, or were religious who had consecrated their whole lives to God's service. Lay people aspired to be good; if martyred they would be saints, otherwise sainthood was for 'the professionals'.

Now here was this middle-aged layman encouraging everyone to be a saint and saying that holiness wasn't difficult. Wojtyła was entranced—and thrilled. Thanks to his father he already had a deep personal faith and knew the importance of regular prayer but Tyranowski was urging him to go deeper.

As one means of instruction, Tyranowski required that all his group kept a notebook with ruled columns and heading, such as ' Scripture', 'Morning/Evening Prayer', 'Afternoon Recreation' and each day the columns were filled in with a tick or a cross. Every moment of the day was organised for either activity or relaxation, spiritual exercises, Mass, scripture reading ranked alongside one's daily duties in life. Tyranowski's motto was 'every moment must be used for something'.

One can see a meticulous accountant's mind behind it all. The rather manly 'roll call' of good works would have been quickly absorbed by the Captain's son. Perhaps, too, the words on the sundial came to mind— *time flies, eternity remains*; no moment of the day should be wasted. Karol regularly went to see Tyranowski to discuss his notes and give an account of all he had done. This early training, building on his father's example, was the foundation for the future Pope's arduous lifestyle in which he demanded more of himself than of anyone else. Karol never missed his daily devotions. As Pope he wrote of Tyranowski 'He showed me the revelation of a new universe, with his words, his spirituality and the example of a life entirely consecrated to God and, by himself, he represented a new world that I did not know yet. I saw the beauty of a soul revealed by grace'.

Members of the group were expected to undertake spiritual reading in addition to scripture. Tyranowski recommended books on an individual basis depending on personality and level of spiritual advancement. Malinski recalls a book by Adolphe Tanqueray (1854-1932), *The Spiritual Life; a Treatise on Ascetical and Mystical Theology*. Published in 1930, it would have been considered modern in 1940 and was, in fact, a standard textbook in seminaries up to the 1960s. Intended to be accessible to all, this work served as a basic introduction to all the stages and types of prayer. The distinction is made between vocal prayer, expressed in words and gestures; 'saying one's prayers', and mental prayer which is a silent focusing on God and building up of a personal relationship with him. The difference would take a strong hold on the young Wojtyła.

Active mental prayer, such as meditating on an event in the Gospels, was often recommended to devout lay people. Jan Tyranowski taught that more was possible: passive mental prayer, contemplation, in which the soul wordlessly opens itself to God and rests in him.

Tyranowski had begun his own spiritual path with *Mystyka*, by Fr Semenenko, the founder of the Resurrectionists who stress a personal relationship with the Lord. He rapidly absorbed it and moved on to the great

Carmelite mystics, St John of the Cross and St Teresa of Avila.

The Living Rosary thrived; soon there were sixty members, divided into four groups of fifteen with a leader for each, directly answering to Tyranowski. Karol Wojtyła was one of the leaders.

Would a small city parish today be able to recruit so many young people? There are so many more distractions and alternative means of amusement on offer. In war time Poland, there was little else to do in the evening than attend church. That church activities were frowned on by the authorities made them more appealing as a form of unspoken protest. Perhaps this was initially true of some of Tyranowski's group, but whatever motivation that initially led them into church, it is to his credit that he was able to nurture each soul which came to him, according to its capacity and desire for improvement. 'What he tried to teach us was new. He wanted to draw new listeners to this new life. Young people think they know everything ...' wrote Pope John Paul II later. Initially they didn't understand him, because he was teaching a new way of living in Christ. For him, the interior life was everything. In the words of St Paul 'It is no longer I who live but Christ lives in me' (Ga 2: 22-23). Tyranowski's apostolate was to result in eleven vocations.

Karol Wojtyła had received the brown scapular when he was ten years old. From that time on, he never took it off, not even when he was being wheeled into surgery after an assassin's bullet almost took his life. An early scapular of his is on display in the museum dedicated to him in Wadowice, it is very tattered and worn. However, at this time in Krakow, the young Wojtyła was to develop his understanding of Mary's role in the church. The Salesians promote a devotion to Mary Help of Christians and Tyranowski put into his hands a work by St Louis Grignion de Montfort who taught 'To Jesus through Mary' through total consecration to Mary.

> At one point I began to question my devotion to Mary, believing that, if it became too great, it might end up compromising the supremacy of the worship owed to Christ. At that time I was greatly helped by a book by St Louis Marie Grignion de Montfort entitled *Treatise of True Devotion to the Blessed Virgin*. There I found the answers to my questions. Yes, Mary does bring us closer to Christ; she does lead us to him, provided that we live her mystery in Christ ... I then came to understand why the Church says the Angelus three times a day ... Such powerful words! They express the deepest reality of the greatest event ever to take place in human history.
>
> This is the origin of the motto *Totus Tuus*. The phrase comes from St Louis de Montfort. It is an abbreviation of a more complete form of entrustment to the Mother of God which runs like this: *totus tuus ego sum et omnia mea tua sunt. Accipio te in mea omnia. Praebe mihi cor tuum, Maria.* (I belong entirely to you, and all that I have is yours. I take you for my all. O Mary, give me your heart'.[4]

As a child, Karol had loved to listen to the singing of the Hours of the Blessed Virgin in church, but until he read de Montfort he never realised the full depth of their meaning. Suddenly the words of Christmas carols and Lenten hymns concerning Mary had greater depth and a richer theological content than he had understood before. 'These spiritual experiences were fundamental in shaping that journey of prayer and contemplation which gradually brought me to the priesthood and which would later continue to guide me in all the events of my life.'

In 2000, addressing a Marian conference in Rome, the Holy Father said 'Then I understood that I could not exclude the Lord's mother from my life without neglecting the will of God-Trinity who willed to begin and fulfil the great mysteries of the history of salvation with the responsible and faithful collaboration of the humble handmaid of Nazareth.' From childhood he had made pilgrimages to Kalwaria Zebzrydowska and later as bishop he would return: 'I would go there often, walking along its paths in solitude and presenting to the Lord in prayer the various problems of the Church, especially in the difficult times during the struggle against communism.'[5]

Heavily influenced by Carmelite spirituality himself, Tyranowski soon discerned that young Karol was ready for John of the Cross. Not an easy read, the works of St John of the Cross deal with the longing of the soul for God, expressed in poetry and prose. As a poet himself, Wojtyła was enchanted, and a delight and fascination for St John remained with him all his life. His first doctoral thesis would be on Faith in John of the Cross.

John of the Cross is often dismissed as too negative and dismal for modern readers but the truth is quite the opposite. Renunciation, self-denial and detachment from created things help to free the soul to love God, other people and creation in the way that God intended. Desire for possessions leads to a spiritual poverty and cuts us off from the graces that God wants to give us. Other people, the created world, even 'things' are all good, but our desire for them dampens our spiritual hunger for God. For John absolutely nothing else matters as much as having God. His way of renunciation is in fact a total abandonment of everything that is not God. However, by giving up everything, the soul finds itself liberated and able to love everything at a much deeper level.

> In detachment from things [human beings] acquire a clearer knowledge of them and a better understanding of both natural and super-natural truths concerning them. Their joy, con-sequently, in those temporal goods is far different from the joy of one who is attached to them and they receive great benefits and advan-tages from their joy. They delight in these goods according to the truth in them, but those who are attached delight in the ... substance of them ... those, then whose joy is unpossessive of things rejoice in them all as though they pos-sessed them all; cares do not molest the detached, neither in prayer or out of it.[6]

In these lines we can see how Karol Wojtyła's lack of possessions and carefulness with food stems from a desire to have more of God. This is not a form of spiritual athleticism, though as an athlete the future pope may have taken seriously the idea of training via self-denial. He certainly took John's advice literally. One day he arrived for work at the Solway chemical plant blue with cold, having given his jacket to a vagrant. As a priest and bishop he was notorious for giving away clothing, sometimes items that had been made lovingly for him. His will, written and revised several times throughout his papacy, states 'I leave no possessions of which it will be necessary to dispose'.

The grim days of the Nazi occupation would bring a detachment of another kind; in 1940 his father died at the age of sixty one. Never entirely well since they moved to Krakow, the Captain's rheumatism was worsened by the dark, damp apartment and he died of a heart attack while Karol was away at work. His son was desolate—the last remaining close relative was gone, and he had died alone. Karol wept and prayed at the bedside all night, inconsolable. It is reported that shortly before his death, the Captain had said to his son: 'I will not live long and would like to be certain before I die that you will commit yourself to God's service'—at no time had the father ever pressed the idea of priesthood on his son, but, ever serious about spiritual matters, he wanted to be sure that Karol would not waste his considerable gifts on temporal and passing things. Friends noted that Karol seemed more serious than before; he was certainly friendly and outgoing in his old manner but there was a deeper gravity about him. He began to think deeply about his life so far, what he had learned and the course of his future life. 'At twenty I had already lost all the people I loved' he would later say. 'God was, in a way, preparing me for what would happen ... After my father's death I became aware of my true path. I was working at a plant and devoting myself, as far as the terrors of the occupation allowed, to my taste in literature and drama. My priestly vocation took place in the midst of all that—I knew that I was called with absolute clarity.'[7]

In fact it took a year and a half from his father's death before his vocation was fully discerned.

Notes

1   For a fuller description of life in Poland under occupation, see C. Wolkowinska and J. Bogle, *When the Summer Ended* (Leominster: Gracewing, 1992).
2   John Paul II, *Gift and Mystery* (New York: Image/Doubleday, 1996), p. 23.
3   M. Malinski, *Pope John Paul II: The Life of my friend Karol Wojtyła* (London: Burns and Oates, 1979), p. 19.
4   John Paul II, *Gift and Mystery* (New York: Image/Doubleday, 1966), p. 30.
5   *Ibid.*, pp. 30–31.
6   St John of the Cross, *Ascent of Mount Carmel,* quoted in M. Foley (ed.), *John of The Cross The Ascent to Joy* (New York: New City Press, 2002), p. 62.
7   A. Frossard, *Be Not Afraid! André Frossard in conversation with John Paul II* (London: Bodley Head, 1984), p. 13.

3

VOCATION AND PRIESTHOOD

 NCE KAROL'S MIND was made up, there was no going back. In vain his actor friends argued with him that he was hiding his talents under a bushel; that he would reach far more people as an actor than ever he would as a priest. If it seemed that way in 1942, the future would prove very different.

No one can claim a priestly vocation without a feeling that it is God himself who is calling. But an interior call does not usually happen without exterior events seeming to confirm it. Friends of Wojtyła have put forward three main factors which probably determined the decision. Tyranowski's guidance in the spiritual life was almost certainly the first, which helped Karol understand that prayer lies at the heart of the Christian's life, then there was the appalling treatment of Jews at the quarry and the Solvay factory; they were brought in each day from a nearby camp at Plaszow. Brought up in an atmosphere of friendship and mutual respect with Jews, Karol must have felt a determination to participate in rebuilding a moral society once the occupation was over. Finally, the death of his father removed the last family tie on earth, leaving him free to give himself entirely to the service of others.

Karol was accepted as a seminarian and began his studies in secret. Fortunately by then he was no longer labouring in the quarry but working in the Solvay chemical factory, a much less physically demanding job. During the long shifts he would find plenty of time to study, his co-workers often covering for him. In fact, many of them already referred to him as 'the little priest' on account of his openly devout practices such as kneeling in prayer on the factory floor.

The secret seminary, with candidates living in their own homes, could only operate with difficulty and became increasingly dangerous, so two years later, Cardinal Sapieha, Archbishop of Krakow, ordered all his seminarians to live with him in the Bishop's residence. Karol Wojtyła was to spend most of his time in the Bishop's capacious dining room on the first floor where he would sleep, eat, attend lectures, pray and study. He was very relieved to be there—some months earlier he had been knocked down by a German truck and left for dead, only surviving through the help of a passer-by. The day before entering the Bishop's house he narrowly avoided being captured in a German round-up of Polish males, most of whom were never seen again. Surviving these experiences must have confirmed to him that God did want him to be a priest after all.[1]

Although he later regretted that he was deprived of a normal seminary experience there is no doubt that he learned a great deal from the clandestine education provided by Cardinal Sapieha. The psychological pressure of knowing that if discovered all his class-mates would suffer the same fate as their friend Jerzy Zachuta, shot by the Gestapo days before the seminary moved to the Archbishop's residence, would equip the new priests with the strength needed to provide pastoral care under the Communists. Having to live so closely alongside others would no doubt have presented its own problems, but learning to manage and get on with differing characters is a skill essential to the priesthood.

Study had no terrors for the young Wojtyła; he would relish it for the rest of his life. He impressed his teachers and fellow students alike by his diligence. When he had struggled, as he did initially with metaphysics—a subject that seemed well nigh impossible under the factory lights at Solvay when he wrestled with a dense textbook—he simply worked harder in order to understand, and the understanding came to him. The prayer to the Holy Spirit that his father had given him must have come in useful—his advice to fellow students who were struggling was to 'sigh to God' for understanding. It was during this time that he set out to learn Spanish by way of a German-Spanish dictionary which was all he had to hand, in order to read John of the Cross in the original. Despite his intellectual gifts, he was not resented by his classmates; his natural sociability made him universally liked. He enjoyed the company of his companions and organised reunions up to the time he left to assume the papacy. Even as a bishop, he never pulled rank or expected any deference at these meetings.

Karol was ordained on November 1st 1946 in the Bishop's private chapel. The following day he said his first Mass in St Leonard's crypt, in Wawel cathedral. He chose this place to emphasise his solidarity with Polish history and the great people buried there, who include St Stanislaw, Father of the Polish nation, whose remains are enclosed in a huge silver casket.

Pope John Paul II's refrain 'Do not be afraid!' was refined among some of the most terrifying experiences imaginable. To rise above such suffering—loss of family, country and friends—required conversion at the deepest level. The exhortation continued with 'open wide the doors to Christ!'—the key to the kind of fearlessness the Pope had in mind. Or as Scripture has it 'There is no fear in love, but perfect love casts out fear. For fear has to do with punishment, and he who fears is not perfected in love' (1 Jn 4:18). To experience this radical transformation, not only must the heart be completely open to the indwelling of the Holy Spirit, but the will of God must be accepted and welcomed; it is a supreme test of faith. Throughout his priestly life, Wojtyła would stress that our duty is to 'find out the will of God for me at this moment'. As we have seen, this desire for, and acceptance of God's will was learned by Karol from early youth onwards.

If Karol's spiritual and priestly formation was untypical for his time—the clandestine seminary, strong lay role-models—Fr Wojtyła's understanding of the priesthood would remain traditional and ortho-dox. The priesthood was a calling, not a career: 'there was a clear sense that what I heard in my heart was no human voice, nor was it first an idea of my own. Christ was calling me to serve him as a priest'.[2] His response was total giving of self; the priest gives himself radi-cally to the service of God in his Church in the way couples give of themselves to each other in marriage. Wojtyła was to meditate a great deal on human love, but as was his way, he never asked of others what he was unwilling to do himself.

Cardinal Sapieha liked to send his most able stu-dents to study in Rome with the advice that they should travel as much as possible. This would take them outside the restricted world imposed by the Communists and show how Christian life was lived elsewhere. Shortly after ordination, Fr Wojtyła went to Rome to study for his first doctorate, on John of the Cross. He also had the opportunity to travel across

Europe, and in France he encountered the Worker Priest movement. His own experiences as a manual labourer among the kind of people he would not ordinarily have come across gave him a privileged insight into the needs and strengths of working people. These experiences would find ultimate fruition in his 1981 encyclical *Laborem Exercens* in which he described the necessity and dignity of human work and the rights of workers to a just wage, humane working hours and freedom of association. His support for the Solidarity movement in Poland stemmed not from a politicised patriotism, but a philosophical and spiritual understanding of the meaning of work and the injustice of exploitation whether from the right or left.

While in France, the new priest made a visit to Ars, the parish where St John Vianney (1786-1859) worked tirelessly in the confessional. The Curé d'Ars had been a simple priest with limited intellectual abilities; he found learning difficult, especially Latin, raising doubts about whether he should be ordained at all. He was eventually sent to a remote rural parish of under three hundred souls which he transformed through personal example and many hours in the confessional. In time people came from all over France to confess to him. Newly-ordained Fr Wojtyła made a vow that he, too, would be a prisoner of the confessional. On arriving at his first parish assignment, he bent to kiss the ground, a gesture used by the Curé d'Ars that Pope John Paul II would make his own on his many pilgrimages around the world.

If Fr Wojtyła's understanding and love of the priesthood deepened over time, his vision of it remained constant. His first assignment, as a curate in the rural parish of Niegowic, about fifteen miles east of Krakow, would set a pattern that would be repeated and refined throughout the rest of his life. His first action after kissing the ground was to seek the chapel where he prostrated himself in prayer before introducing himself to the parish priest. Before long he had set up a Living Rosary and a drama group for youth. He taught the children catechism in schools and set up a marriage preparation group for engaged couples. He was a frequent visitor to people's homes, his under-standing of human labour gaining respect from the farming community in which he now lived. In order to keep fit, he sometimes joined the workers in the fields. Their respect for him increased when they learned that this bright young man fresh from Rome was living a spartan life similar to their own. He slept on a bare bed and had no more luxuries than they did. He shared everything he had with those who had less. His crowning achievement was to replace the wooden church with a brick one which exists to this day.

All this activity might look like the work of a hyper-active temperament; the seeds of it however lay elsewhere. Fr Wojtyła poured out all his energies in response to the call he had received. At its heart lay the sacraments, as he never tired of explaining:

> The priestly vocation is essentially a call to sanc-tity in the form that derives from the sacrament of Holy Orders. Sanctity is intimacy with God; it is the imitation of Christ, poor, chaste and humble; it is unreserved love for souls and self-giving to their true good; it is love for the church which is holy and wants us to be holy ... each one of you must be holy also in order to help your brothers pursue their vocation in sanctity.[3]

For Wojtyła, the priesthood was to be lived alongside the people he served. He had learned that priests should not be a separate caste of remote spiritual elites and clericalism was never a temptation for him. On the contrary, he believed that a priest should be able to converse on a variety of topics, from science to jazz, so that he could be with people 'in everything but sin'.

It was at the Mass that the priest functioned more visibly, acting towards those he served 'in persona Christi' (in the person of Christ). In contrast to more recently-coined notions of the priest as 'celebrant' or 'presider', Wojtyła upheld the traditional description of the priest at Mass is an *alter Christus* (another Christ); 'the priesthood in its deepest reality is the priesthood of Christ. It is Christ who offers himself, his Body and Blood in sacrifice to God the Father and by this sacrifice makes righteous in the Father's eyes all mankind and indirectly all creation ... for this reason the celebration of the Eucharist must be the most important moment of the priest's day, the centre of his life'.[4] For Wojtyła, the Mass was the pivotal moment of the day around which everything else revolved. It must be approached in a spirit of prayer—he himself would pray for some time before saying Mass so he could approach the altar in a state of complete recollection; as Pope, recalls one server, he could be vested while kneeling, holding out his arms with his eyes still closed. After Mass he always spent time in making a thanksgiving.

If he was nothing if not traditional in his understanding of the priesthood as a partaking in the priesthood of Christ, with its implications of servanthood, suffering and victory (St Paul's 'more than conquerors'), Fr Wojtyła was not averse to saying Mass in unusual places: in the mountains while hiking with young people, an upturned kayak as an altar with two paddles tied together in a cross. Even today some might feel uncomfortable with this, but in a world where spies were everywhere and priests were forbidden from consorting with young people, new solutions had to be found.

Mindful of his promise at Ars, Wojtyła regularly heard confessions, even as bishop and as Pope when he would sit in the confessionals in St Peter's Basilica during Holy Week. As a young priest in Krakow, he would spend an hour or more with individuals if he felt this was needed. For him, the sacrament was not just a means of reeling off a list of sins or talking through problems as a kind of therapeutic encounter, but a means of growing in grace through wise discernment. If the end result was not a growth in holiness, then the exercise was, well, just an exercise. He could be demanding, expecting the same high standards in his penitents as he did from himself; as Pope he would go to confession weekly.

Never judgmental, he helped each individual to see his or her own life as part of the will of God—his advice, 'you must decide' left the choice open. Mature faith demands a personal response to a dilemma, given guidance when asked for but never force. The adage that everyone is called to be a saint remained close to his heart and he would accompany each person for as far as they needed in the quest for holiness.

He developed the art of listening; a difficult and tiring skill to acquire. It is easy to sit silently, just letting the other person ramble on; but people who met Pope John Paul II all remarked on how he made them feel as if they were the only person that mattered at that moment. Listening, accompanying the other, was one aspect of Wojtyła's self-giving as a priest, and he gave generously.

Throughout his life, Wojtyła never stopped wondering at the 'gift and mystery' which was the priesthood. He felt totally fulfilled by it. At the time his vocation was made clear, Karol seems to have had some kind of infused understanding of the demands of celibacy. And following that, as if to confirm it: 'A day came when I knew for certain that my life would not be fulfilled in the human love the beauty of which I have always felt deeply'.[5]

From his earliest days as a priest, Fr Wojtyła had an special love of young people; he prepared them for marriage, blessed their homes and baptised their children. There was nothing that he would not discuss. For him the married state was not in opposition to, but complementary to virginity and celibacy. The two converge in the renunciation of the individual self, existing in and for itself.

When he heard that a priest had written a book purporting to show that he, Karol Wojtyła, had been sexually active before his ordination, Pope John Paul II responded with fierce denial, angry and grieved that a fellow priest should make such assertions, as if it were not possible for a normal young man to resist temptations to purity. At the time of his election to the Chair of Peter, there were rumours of his having had a girlfriend as proof of his 'normality'. In fact, there is no evidence to support this at all. The main candidate chosen by commentators was a young woman who took part in plays with Karol, but she has always denied any romance. In any case, a young man brought up in pre-war Poland, in the 'domestic seminary' of his parental home, is likely to have been very serious in his attitude to relationships. Thus he knew that the discipline of celibacy was possible and indeed could be normal for an unattached young man.

In conversation with André Frossard, he said

> Christ asked of us purity of heart according to our station in life and our vocation. He demands it squarely. But what is more, he shows us the way to values which are only revealed to the pure vision and the pure heart. We cannot acquire this purity without renunciation, without inner struggles against our own weakness; but, once acquired, this maturity of heart and mind makes up a hundredfold for the efforts which it rewards. The result is a new spontaneity of feeling, of gesture and of behaviour which facilitates relations with people, especially with children.[6]

Purity of heart leads, not to cold isolation, but a greater depth of encounter with others.

Throughout his life, Karol Wojtyła reached out to the young. As a pastor in Krakow or a university professor dealing with students, he organised debates, respecting the opinions of others before replying. When a young Marxist student interrupted one of his lectures with a strident denunciation of Christian principles, the young professor listened silently before responding that the young man showed that he had begun to think. By engaging with him rather than reprimanding, Fr Wojtyła encouraged deeper discussion. The young man eventually became a priest.

Later, as Pope, John Paul II began the World Youth Days, usually held biannually, which attracted and challenged hundreds of thousands of young people from all over the world. He had been warned that no one would be interested, the things of God were not 'cool' and young people would only travel to large stadiums to hear rock bands, not an ageing celibate. The detractors were wrong—World Youth Day was one of the most successful initiatives of a papacy remarkable for bold and creative thinking. Vocations were nurtured, friendships found and many marriages ensued from the events in which the message was always the same: Christ is the answer to your problems, in him is the fulfilment that you seek, even if you don't yet know it.

From his father, he had learned about human fatherhood, from Father Figlewicz and Cardinal Sapieha he had seen the model of a good priestly father, thus Pope John Paul II developed a father's heart for the whole world. At the time of his death even non-Catholics declared that they had lost their holy father too. In his priestly life, lived as 'another Christ', he had expanded his heart to encompass all of humanity, including the millions who do not follow Christ. After the assassination attempt of 1981, it seemed to the Holy Father that the life miraculously restored to him was no longer his own. As St Paul wrote 'It is no longer I who live, but Christ lives in me' (Ga 2:20). From then on he would offer himself every moment as a 'living sacrifice' in imitation of the Eucharist that is offered every day at Mass.

Self-sacrifice is part of the dying to self required of a priest, sometimes literally; as Christ said 'the good shepherd lays down his life for his sheep'. A good example of this was Fr Maximilian Maria Kolbe, the Franciscan priest who, interned in the concentration camp at Auschwitz, offered to change places with a family man who had been condemned to death by starvation. Fr Kolbe, a Pole, was canonised by Pope John Paul II who held him in the highest esteem, calling him 'the patron saint of our difficult century'.

Much of Wojtyła's spare time before becoming Pope was spent in the company of lay people, and he had, as we have seen, a unique insight into the role of the laity, thanks to the example of holy people. His ideas looked forward to the theme of the universal call to holiness that would be one of the strongest messages from the Second Vatican Council. However, almost from the outset of his papacy, John Paul knew that he must encourage his fellow priests. If some believed that the increasing shortage of priests was a disguised blessing intended by God to call the laity to greater responsibility in the Church, Wojtyła did not. He viewed the exodus of so many from the priesthood with dismay and sorrow. As a bishop, concerned about the number of priests in his diocese, he had promised Our Lady that he would visit, on foot, all her pilgrimage sites within reach of Krakow if she sent one seminarian each time. This seemed to work, as vocations grew and the seminaries in his diocese were soon thriving. It is also worth recalling the adage that good bishops bring vocations!

So as Pope, John Paul began the annual letters to priests, sent every Holy Thursday throughout his papacy, apart from 1981. These exhortations, always addressed to his 'brother priests' sought to rekindle the joy and enthusiasm within the priestly vocation. Being a priest was the most worthwhile calling possible with the facility to celebrate the Eucharist, to feed the spiritually hungry, to work for souls: in short, to be other Christs to the world, bringing the world to Christ.

A priest must be a man of the word and an evangeliser. He cannot proclaim the word unless he lives it first. If God's word is not to return empty (Is 55:11), the messenger must be prepared. This is not done by sophisticated parish programs, but by priestly holiness which alone will reap spiritual fruit. If the Mass is the centre of each day, its fruits are nurtured by prayer and meditation. In addition, every priest is required to pray the breviary, the Divine Office, daily and Wojtyła was faithful to this all his life. As he came round from the operation to remove the bullet that almost killed him, his first words were 'Have we said Compline yet?'

Notes

1   For a detailed description of all this, see G. Weigel, *Witness to Hope* (New York and London: HarperCollins, 1999), pp. 69–72.
2   John Paul II, *Address to young people,* Los Angeles (15 September 1987).
3   John Paul II, *Address to priests*, Rome (9 October 1984).
4   John Paul II, *Gift and Mystery* (New York: Image/Doubleday, 1996), p. 75.
5   A. Frossard, *Be Not Afraid! André Frossard in conversation with John Paul II* (London: Bodley Head, 1984), p. 16.
6   *Ibid.*

4

MARY: 'TOTUS TUUS', THE 'FATIMA POPE'

WHEN THE SUBJECT of John Paul's devotion to Mary comes up in a discussion, almost invariably someone will announce confidently that 'of course' this devotion was rooted in the fact that he lost his mother at a very young age. The claim is that Mary became a substitute figure and this, combined with a strong sense of Poland's Marian traditions, produced the Marian theme which echoed so strongly throughout John Paul's adult life and deeply influenced his pontificate.

But the reality is rather different. John Paul's Marian theology is profoundly bound up with his theology of the Church—his understanding of the strong bond between the two. And this is in turn rooted in a deep personal devotion to Mary that is centred in his Christology rather than in any psychological need.

Certainly, the young Karol Wojtyła grew up in a Catholic environment where devotion to Mary was taken for granted: an image of Mary was in every Catholic home, and a sodality of Mary in every Catholic school. The image of Our Lady of Czestochowa would have been familiar to him from early childhood, part of the everyday fabric of life, as familiar as a crucifix, or as the Polish eagle on a public building. He would have learned the 'Hail Mary' and 'Hail Holy Queen' along with other prayers like the 'Our Father' and the 'Glory be ...' and would have seen and heard his parents praying the Rosary.

And, certainly, after the deaths of his mother and his older brother Edmund, it would have been to the Rosary as a prayer of hope and consolation that he and his father would have turned, praying it together in the family home where now just the two of them were left together.

But the deepening of Karol Wojtyła's Marian devotion came, not in childhood with his mother's death but, as we have seen (Chapter 2) in early adulthood, with the discovery of St Louis Grignion de Montfort's book on *True Devotion to Mary*.

Many years later, he would express in poetry something of the bond between Mary and her Son, in 'Her Amazement at her only Child', imagining Mary writing:

> I knew: the light that lingered in ordinary things,
> Like a spark sheltered under the skin of our days—
> The light was you;
> It did not come from me.
> And I had more of you in that luminous silence
> Than I had of you as the fruit of my body, my blood.[1]

The Madonna of Częstochowa, Poland's national icon, is no blonde maiden with rosy cheeks and a simpering smile. The icon is of great antiquity—one tradition claims it was painted by St Luke—and it shows Mary with solemn forward gaze, holding her Divine son, her face with its two slash-marks sombre—even severe—surrounded by a dark mantle spangled with stars, with a great golden halo beyond. Our Lady of Częstochowa is a figure of solemnity, of suffering, but also of tenderness and of power. Here is someone who understands sorrow and trouble, who takes up burdens, who lifts prayers and supplications to God. Poles have prayed to her in all the struggles of their national history, and in their family and personal lives. For John Paul, intercession to Mary was something manly and whole-some, associated with watching his father pray and sharing the Rosary with him, and associated too with Poland's history and with the dark times of his own youth when invasion and war brought so much horror.

John Paul's encyclical *Redemptoris Mater* taught about Mary in a rich theological way. In it, he links two great moments in which the Holy Spirit intervened in human history: at Nazareth, when God became incar-nate in Mary's womb, and at Pentecost, when the Spirit descended upon the gathered Church. Throughout his pontificate, John Paul always showed a strong sense of the importance of time: of God at work in history, of Christ as the Lord of time. The mystery of God being incarnate in a woman's womb is something he sees as very much bound up with this, and he focuses on the Scriptural message that it was 'in the fullness of time' that the Angel Gabriel brought the news to Mary. With the tradition of the Church, he sees Mary as the 'morning star' that precedes the dawn—and with his own strong sense of God being in charge of history, he linked this with a fresh need to examine the role of Mary in the light of a coming new Millennium.

For John Paul, life was always a drama—not in the sense of a series of exciting incidents or a need to make a great fuss over every sort of event, but in the real sense of God intervening in history, and man co-operating with God in the drama of salvation. His understanding of the role of Mary is permeated with this, and it became tangible in his own life with the drama of the assassination attempt on 13 May 1981, and its link with the Marian apparitions at Fatima. The gunman who fired the shots at John Paul that day in St Peter's Square was a paid assassin. Given the political realities of the time, the obvious paymasters are the Communist rulers of the then Soviet Union and its satellite states. They—and whoever else was involved in the attempted killing—had failed to understand that God too is at work in history, and has his own mysterious purposes.

As John Paul was rushed to hospital—he lost six pints of blood and the bullet caused five wounds in his intestines, missing the main abdominal artery by a hair's breadth—he was heard praying 'Mary, my mother ...'

The day, 13 May, was the anniversary of the apparitions of Mary at Fatima in Portugal in 1917, the year that the Bolsheviks took power in Russia, enforcing Communism and establishing the Soviet Union. At Fatima Mary had appeared to three children and asked for prayers and penance, promising that if this happened, 'Russia' would be converted.

Uncomprehending—they did not know who or what 'Russia' was—they faithfully reported this and began to offer prayers and penances as the vision had requested. Thus began the drama of 'Our Lady of Fatima' which captured the attention of Catholics worldwide over the next decades. By the 1960s and 70s, 'Fatima devotions' were an established part of life in Catholic culture, and the shrine built at the site of the apparitions in Portugal was attracting vast crowds annually. The feast of Our Lady of Fatima was established as 13 May, and the significance of the date was something that John Paul would have grasped at once.

Lying in hospital recovering from the shots that had so nearly killed him, John Paul sent for the Fatima papers from the Vatican archives. These included the famous 'Third Secret', the final document which had not yet been made public. Its contents must have shaken him considerably: it revealed that the children had seen a vision of a 'Bishop dressed in white—we had the impression it was the Holy Father' being shot and falling to the ground, as the climax of a vision of many martyrs and a landscape of suffering and ruins dominated by a great rugged cross. John Paul would later reveal this Secret, to worldwide publicity, in the year 2000. Meanwhile, in 1982 he went to Fatima a year after the assassination attempt and the bullet that should have ended his life was placed in Mary's crown—where it fitted perfectly. John Paul was never in any doubt that Mary had saved his life: 'One hand fired the bullet, another guided it'.

The thanksgiving Mass at Fatima was a magnificent occasion, attended by a vast crowd of the faithful from across Portugal and from all over the world. In a minor but notable addition to the drama, a priest from the Lefebvrist sect, opposed to the teachings of the Second Vatican Council, rushed to attack John Paul, lunging at him with a knife. He drew blood but did no lasting damage.

John Paul II was 'the Pope of Fatima'. In 1984 he consecrated the world—including Russia of course—to Mary's Immaculate Heart. In 2000 when the full 'Third Secret' was revealed, the Church and the world could ponder the images in the children's vision and the great events of the twentieth century. By then, Communism had collapsed, and Russia's conversion to Christianity was becoming evident to all as churches reopened and processions and icons and the calendar of Christian feasts and seasons reappeared in Russian life.

John Paul commissioned Cardinal Joseph Ratzinger, then Prefect of the Congregation for the Doctrine of the Faith, to produce a theological commentary on the images in the Third Secret, which he duly did.[2]

Today a small marble square in the piazza at St Peter's marks the place where John Paul fell on 13 May 1981—and as you look up, you see an image of Mary, with the inscription 'Totus Tuus' high on the wall beyond.

For John Paul, Mary was always at once an intimate intercessor and a great theological reality. She was a central player in the drama of the Incarnation, but also a mother to every human being who calls on her for aid, and the patroness of special causes and of nations. She exemplifies a 'yes' to the will of God—and in this she is both a model for the Church and a forerunner of the Church.

For John Paul, Mary was never an 'extra' for Christians, but always at the core, the heart, of the Faith. And it in this sense that she is a pattern for the Church. This was, of course, the message of *Lumen Gentium* (1964), the Vatican II document on the Church which devotes an entire section specifically to Mary. There had been considerable debate at the Second Vatican Council about whether or not to have a document specifically on Mary, and many commentators—then and in the post-Conciliar years—stated that the decision not to do so, and to incorporate Marian theology into the document into the document on the Church, was a way of 'downgrading' Mary.

John Paul would never allow this approach to be taken, and instead he developed his own strong

emphasis on Mary: her pre-eminent role in the drama
of salvation, her ongoing role in the life of the Church,
her motherly presence among Christians, her special
tenderness towards people and nations in need. He
went further, teaching a 'Marian profile' of the Church,
a Church open to God's will, journeying in hope. In
1987 in an address to the Roman Curia he spoke of this
'Marian profile' of the Church, a profile which emphasised discipleship and a readiness to be formed into
sanctity 'in line with the ideal of sanctity already
programmed and prefigured in Mary'.[3] This is a richer
image of the Church than that of a structure with rules
and systems, or of a 'perfect society' with everything
in place and instructions to preserve it. As his biographer George Weigel would note 'The message was
unmistakeable. Discipleship came before authority in
the Church and sanctity came before power, even the
apostolically transmitted priestly power...' [4] John
Paul's 'Marian profile' of the Church builds on *Lumen
Gentium* and assumes an understanding of authority
perceived as service.

John Paul did not invent this concept of a 'Marian
profile'—his study of the subject flowed from the work
of Hans Urs von Balthasar and Henri de Lubac,[5] both
of whom had long been writing about the missing
Marian dimension of ecclesiology. His voice now gave
strength to this. The Marian approach gave a fresh
dimension to the discussion about the nature of the
Church. It challenged the pyramid-hierarchical per-
spective that had dominated in the nineteenth century
and the first half of the twentieth, and it also challenged the vision of a somewhat bureaucratic and
committee-led Church which, in the 1980s and 90s, at

diocesan level too often seemed to have plenty of salaried officials but a poor devotional life.

Mary as the unique work of God, Mary as interces-sor, Mary as the tabernacle carrying the Lord in safety for us, harbouring him for us ... these are all themes in John Paul's own devotional life as well as in the teaching he gives in *Redemptoris Mater* and elsewhere.

John Paul will always be very much associated with the Rosary: he became the first Pope ever to make a popular recording, and a CD of his recitation of the Rosary in Latin, interspersed with music, became a best-seller. The Rosary had always been important for him. In 2002, issuing a special document on the subject he reminisced:

> From my youthful years this prayer has held an important place in my spiritual life. I was powerfully reminded of this during my recent visit to Poland, and in particular at the Shrine of Kalwaria. The Rosary has accompanied me in moments of joy and in moments of difficulty. To it I have entrusted any number of concerns; in it I have always found comfort ...[6]

In this document, *Rosarium Virginis Mariae*, he startled the world by introducing five new Mysteries to the Rosary, thus filling in a 'gap' that previously been present, in that the Mysteries offered for meditation the events of Christ's Incarnation and childhood but then went on directly to his Passion, without any reference to his adult life, miracles or teaching. The Luminous Mysteries were offered, John Paul emphasised, merely as an option—they quickly became popular and are now included in all standard lists of Mysteries of the Rosary.

In explaining the importance of the Rosary, John Paul gave a glimpse into his own interior life:

The Rosary mystically transports us to Mary's side as she is busy watching over the human growth of Christ in the home of Nazareth. This enables her to train us and to mould us with the same care, until Christ is 'fully formed' in us (cf. Ga 4:19). This role of Mary, totally grounded in that of Christ and radically subordinated to it, 'in no way obscures or diminishes the unique mediation of Christ, but rather shows its power' (*Lumen Gentium*, 20). This is the luminous principle expressed by the Second Vatican Council which I have so powerfully experienced in my own life and have made the basis of my episcopal motto: *Totus Tuus*.[7]

Notes

1   John Paul II, *The Place Within — the Poetry of Pope John Paul II* (London: Hutchinson, 1982), p. 43.

2   Congregation for the Doctrine of the Faith, *The Message of Fatima* (13 May 2000). The document includes photostatic reproductions of Lucia's own handwritten account on a sheet of old-fashioned fourfold notepaper, together with a full account of the Fatima visions, and Cardinal Ratzinger's detailed commentary. See the link www.vatican.va/roman_curia/congregations/cfaith/documents/rc_con_cfaith_doc_20000626_message-fatima_en.html.

3   John Paul II, *Annual Address to the Roman Curia*, 22 December 1987 in *L'Osservatore Romano*, English Language edition (11 January 1988).

4   G. Weigel, *Witness to Hope: The Biography of Pope John Paul II* (New York and London: HarperCollins, 1999), p. 577.

5   See, for example, H. de Lubac, *The Motherhood of the Church* (San Francisco: Ignatius, 1982).

6   John Paul II, *Rosarium Virginis Mariae* (2002), 2.

7   *Ibid.*, 15.

POLAND: 'FROM WHICH MY HEART CAN NEVER BE DETACHED'

 HERE IS A story about Pope John Paul asking a little Polish girl 'Where is Poland?' The child was puzzled and didn't reply. The Pope gently tapped her heart and said 'Here. Here is Poland.'[1] Love of country is a matter of the heart. It belongs there with love of parents, and love of neighbour, and it carries some of the same duties and responsibilities.

Cardinal Stephan Wysziński used to like to describe a nation as 'a family of families'. Neither he nor John Paul had any time for fervent nationalism, much less any hint of racialism. Patriotism involved love of neighbour, duties towards the common good, a sense of gratitude to God for blessings received, and a knowledge of the importance of sharing these.

John Paul learned his patriotism from his father, who had served in the army of Austria-Hungary in its last days, and later in the Army of newly-independent Poland. Wadowice, the town where the Wojtyłas lived, belonged to that part of Poland which had been in the Empire, under the Habsburg monarchs. The Poles were strongly Polish, but they had an affection for the Habsburg Empire, ruled as it was by a Catholic monarchy and offering, at least in theory, a degree of freedom and local initiative and independence not known in the parts of Poland ruled by Prussia and Russia.

John Paul's father had a particular loyalty to Archduke Karl—later and briefly the last Emperor of

Austria-Hungary. The young Archduke commanded the section of the Austro-Hungarian army in which Wojtyła served. The young Archduke was courageous, honest, and hard-working, with a practical and at the same time visionary approach to the future. He was known to favour a more flexible form of empire, in which nations and language groups would be able to thrive as partners and neighbours: he had outlined this on various occasions, suggesting that some of the countries could even be republics, but bound by common bonds of trade and culture and history, clustered around the Danube.

A devout Catholic, Archduke Karl was married to a Bourbon Princess, Zita. He had not expected to inherit the throne while still young: the assassination of the heir, Archduke Franz Ferdinand, in 1914 not only set off the chain of events leading to the First World War and the shattering impact it would have on so many families and nations, but also changed the course of Karl's life. He inherited the throne in 1916, with the war at its height, and devoted the next two years to seeking peace with the Allies. Denounced and betrayed, he was finally unable to influence the course of events and thousands of young men continued to die until the final Armistice of 1918.[2]

The young Karol Wojtyła, then, grew up with stories of the Habsburg Empire's traditions and its heritage: a Catholic empire in the heart of Europe. He was also steeped in tales of Poland, of Polish saints and heroes, of St Stanislaus the hero-bishop of Krakow, of Queen Jadwiga under whose rule Christianity flourished along with learning and culture and whose marriage to a Lithuanian prince took the Faith to that country, of Jan Sobieski and his defence of Christian Europe threatened by militant Islam.

He was also given an understanding that political and social change did not have to mean the abandonment of good traditions and values. Poland in the 1920s was a new nation with a strong sense of an ancient heritage, and its young people saw themselves as part of a democratic future with new opportunities while cherishing a great history.

A very important part of Karol Wojtyła's understanding of Poland—and of the nature of nationhood, as he came to ponder it and speak of it as a mature priest, Bishop and finally Pope—was that it is culture, not politics and not the rule of the State as such, that drives real history. He never saw the Church as being in fundamental alliance with the State. That might work and it might not, but it was not the only way, or even the best way—and perhaps not the way for the future at all.

Poland had lived in its culture, in families and in community life, in lore and language and customs and traditions, in poetry and prose, even while it did not exist formally on a map. For centuries, the Catholic faith was central to the lives of families, and was shared as the core—literally the heart—of community life.

At the Reformation, Poland did not experience the searing internal conflicts that marked many countries in Europe in the sixteenth and seventeenth centuries. Protestantism was seen as something coming 'from outside' and the Swedish invasion of the 1650s reinforced this. The fact that the Swedish conquest did not last gave Poles a confidence in their own sense of Catholic identity, and this was reinforced by the victory of Jan Sobieski against the Turks at Vienna in 1683.

Poles would develop from all this a strong sense of their
nation as having a special destiny, and later on, in the
nineteenth century after the country had been divided
between Russia, Prussia, and Austria, there was a deep
romantic idea of Poland as the 'Christ among the
nations', suffering for the final good of all, enduring
anguish but looking towards a later resurrection. This
national sense of 'Polish messianism' could even take
quite extreme forms in poetry and literature.[3]

The Polish relationship to the Church was one of the
heart, and also one that linked the Church not with the
State as such but with nationhood as exemplified by
culture, a common history, and great ideals and deeds.
This was subtly different from the classic Church/State
bond on a Catholic monarchy in a Catholic state.

In the nineteenth century, freedom of religion
became an issue for Poles in the Russian empire, where
Catholicism was seen as dangerous to Russian Ortho-
doxy, and under Prussia where the Kulturkampf produced problems. By 1920, when Poland regained
independence and integrity as a nation in its own right,
the Catholic Church was associated with a belief in
freedom and independence, and the Church was loved
and recognised as custodian of culture and national
identity. Establishment of the Church in any formal
sense in government was seen as associated with
foreign rule—even if, as with Austria, that rule had been
on the whole benign. Poles saw the Church as alive in
the nation without any need to impose it and they also
saw elsewhere—for example in America where so
many had settled—a way of being Catholic where the
Church was strong and flourishing in freedom.

On the other hand, there was also a very deeply
developed sense of Poland having a mission, of the

great necessity of the country remaining Catholic and of converting others. Hence a great missionary zeal in the 1920s and 30s, with missionaries going abroad to serve in Africa and Asia—Fr Maximillian Kolbe and his Franciscans in Japan and so on—and with energetic missionary zeal at home, Catholic events and rallies, parish missions, publications, youth groups, and more. A downside of this was preaching against the beliefs of others—usually linking together atheists and Jews and using passionate language in telling them how wrong they were.

To be a Catholic was normal and mainstream, and so the rhythm of family prayer and Sunday Mass, celebrations for feast-days, and the annual round of the Church's calendar, seemed part of the very fabric of things. In the family home, and along the wayside, a crucifix or a shrine to Mary found its natural and accepted place, and was decorated with flowers and used as a stopping-place for prayer.

The Polish Catholicism of the 1920s and 30s drew heavily on the Polish people's sense of history, and when invasion came in 1939—from Nazi Germany in the West and from the Soviets in the East—it would be the Catholic faith that gave many Poles the courage to survive and believe in the possibility of a revived nation in the future.

But Karol Wojtyła's faith as it developed through his young manhood in the grim years of the German occupation—working in a stone quarry, reading and performing plays in an underground theatre group, and then committing himself to the priesthood and training in a secret seminary—was something deeper than the Polish national Catholicism outlined above, and in certain specific ways it rejected some of that national form.

At one level, of course, Karol Wojtyła's faith was very Polish. He was a son of Poland. He was very much a man of place—he loved Wadowice 'where it all began' as he put it. He loved the Tatra mountains where he walked and skied. He loved Krakow, the city where he studied, where in underground drama groups he and other young people kept the flame of Polish culture burning, the city where he became a priest, the city entrusted to his care as Archbishop.

And his Polish Catholicism meant that throughout his life he celebrated, as a matter of course, his name-day—the feast of his patron saint, Charles Borromeo—rather than his birthday. It meant that Polish carols and the breaking of the traditional Christmas wafer, and the vigil meal on Christmas Eve, were a central part of every year. He went on pilgrimages to Polish shrines: walking, praying and singing together as part of a great crowd along a pilgrim route was a standard part of every summer. He had an image of Our Lady of Częstochowa with him in Rome. Poland was always in his heart and in his prayers.

John Paul's own wartime experiences were at one level very Polish: hunger, oppression, daily fear of random arrest, freedom restricted, national identity crushed. Uniquely among the occupied nations in World War II, Poland produced no Quisling government or group that co-operated in any way with the invaders: its opposition groups operated on a wide scale and—especially in the final attempt at an uprising in Warsaw—with great valour. Poland saw not only the general suffering and horror of war, but the particular evils associated with World War II: Auschwitz, with its industrial-scale programmed killing was on Polish soil. When, after the war, the Divine Mercy message emerged in Krakow its message struck home across Poland. Mankind needed God's mercy, because unspeakable evils had taken place at the hands of men and only mercy from a loving God made any sense at all. (This subject will be explored elsewhere in this book, but its Polish origins are of relevance here).

All of this makes John Paul a very Polish figure. But in other ways he transcended any sense of simply sharing a national faith, and he also learned from Poland things that he would later use in unexpected ways. He was not blind to the faults of his fellow-countrymen. His passionate denunciations of anti-Semitism came from a man who knew that this was an issue in Poland. It had existed for centuries, an ugly aspect of Polish life. He himself had lived a different experience: his close friend at school was a Jew and they were welcomed in one another's homes. As Bishop, years later, meeting Jerzy Kluger again brought not only joy to them both but something more important: an opportunity to work together for a whole new Catholic-Jewish understanding with long-term implications. John Paul's Polishness had thus made him aware of an issue that might have escaped the attentions of a Pope from elsewhere, an issue that would be taken up by his successors and be of great significance at a deep level into the future

John Paul was Polish, but his formation began in a Wadowice that had been part of a large European empire and that educated in that tradition. Latin and the classics, the study of the ancient world, European and world history, were all a standard part of his secondary school curriculum. His initial studies—

philosophy and theology—for the priesthood in Krakow were continued at post-graduate level in Rome. And before that, on his own initiative, he had been deeply influenced by the mysticism of Spain's St John of the Cross, and by the writings of France's St Louis Grignion de Montfort.

Throughout his life, John Paul read, wrote and spoke a range of different languages, never confining himself only to books available in Polish. His post-ordination studies gained him a doctorate in Rome after travels which included time with worker-priests in France. As Pope he spoke often of Europe and Europe's Christian soul. But he looked beyond. His style as Pope often had something of the New World about it—World Youth Day and its associated activities, and the vast papal Masses and celebrations on his world trips, owed something to the "big tent" evangelistic missions of American preachers such as Billy Graham, and he was able to appeal to that culture. He was loved in Latin America, where his warmth and sense of joy in his faith meant that he made common cause with the people there. As Pope, he had the ability to connect with people over a wide range of languages and cultures. As a man who had experienced oppression, invasion, and war in his native land, he felt for people who had similarly experienced such things.

Was this partly because the Polish tradition itself includes an openness to the world? By the mid-twentieth century, Polish missionaries had been working in Africa, Asia, and the Americas in great numbers for many years. Polish settlers went to America and to Australia in the nineteenth century and throughout the twentieth. The Second World War saw a Polish diaspora settled around the globe as soldiers made new homes in the USA, Britain, Australia, New Zealand and Southern Africa rather than be forced to live under Stalin's rule. A Polish Pope belonged to a nation which for all sorts of reasons had looked outward for a long time. And while many Poles, in looking outward, sought to retain their own beliefs and to convert others to Catholicism too, there was also inevitably a two-way process in which they absorbed lessons from the places where they settled and worked, discovering that America, for instance, was a place where the Catholic faith could flourish in freedom.

Within Europe, too, Poles had long looked outward, to Paris or to Vienna as well as to Krakow or Warsaw in seeking education or cultural life. Only the imposition of the Iron Curtain and Soviet domination had changed that. There had long been this grim reality of Russia, forcing Poles to look eastwards even when they had no wish to do so—Russia with its grim vastness, where so many Poles were taken against their will, whether in Tsarist times as prisoners following an abortive uprising, or under Communism in the brutal deportations to the gulag or to mass killings at Katyn and elsewhere.

Poland has never been an isolated inward-looking nation: and in the twentieth century, Poland's history was, more than that of most nations, bound up with its neighbours' activities, and with emigration and with war. Poland's history, taught to Karol Wojtyła as a young boy not only in school but by his soldier father, was about great issues: war, battles, faith, endurance, the free exercise of religious practice, the passing-on of values and beliefs and traditions.

John Paul's return to Poland as Pope in 1979 was a great turning-point in the history of the modern world.

Characteristically, he did not take the opportunity to make any political claim: this was a pilgrimage and the message was a spiritual one, an appeal to the nation's soul. 'May the Holy Spirit descend on the land — this land' was the central cry of his great sermon in Warsaw at the great open-air sanctuary created there, addressing vast crowds who had surged there from across the country. A nation renewed in the Holy Spirit would find its own destiny — that was John Paul's conviction. Truth defies lies and errors and will triumph in the end, and it imposes itself by the strength of its own reality. Courage, patience and prayer would open people up for the renewal that God would send.

This was a Polish message for Poles, in a nation which had known conquest, savage foreign rule, deportations and injustice. But it was also a message to the world: that Christ's call is one of hope for everyone and in all places. John Paul did not, essentially, believe in one message for his fellow-countrymen and another for everyone else. His cry in Warsaw was echoed in his cry for the poor in South America or for the consumerist rich of Western Europe or the USA: the Holy Spirit can change things, can renew hearts, can open up a new chapter of hope and love.

Poland was 'a far country', as John Paul put it when he stepped out on to the balcony of St Peter's and addressed the Church and the world for the first time as Pope in 1978. He added that it was a country always close to the heart of the Church in Rome. John Paul's Polish identity rooted him in a Catholic faith that was confident of its own identity, a Catholicism with a strong culture and traditions. It rooted him, too, in a culture influenced by a 'Polish messianism' which believed in a special role for Poland in world history.

But his was a faith that was also intellectually grounded, and capable of providing answers to some of the deepest questions raised by the men and women of a difficult century, a faith that launched the process that led to the collapse of Communism, a faith that spoke to people of every continent and background.

For John Paul, Poland was 'where it all began'. The 'it' of his life went on to include world travels on such a scale that, when the miles were counted up, the figure was the equivalent to a three-times journey to the moon and back, and a final resting-place in Rome visited by huge numbers of pilgrims from every continent. The adventure of his extraordinary life had its beginnings in the faith taught through the traditions and heritage of a people strongly conscious of having received something great that would sustain them through all vicissitudes. To that extent, John Paul was Polish through and through.

In 1979, after his history-making visit to Poland as Pope, John Paul was seen to brush away tears as he took his farewell of his countrymen at Warsaw airport to fly back to Rome. He once again kissed the ground, as he had done on his arrival, the ground, he said 'from which my heart can never be detached'.

Over a decade later, making a pilgrimage to a free Poland, he was visibly concerned about the signs of consumerism and an apparent growing disregard for the spiritual and moral roots of the new-found freedom. But on his final visit, the clear bond that he had with his countrymen, and his ability to speak to their deepest needs, was still as clear as ever. New issues were emerging: how to live as Christians amid new pressures, how to retain a healthy patriotism without becoming nationalistic, how to give a full and convincing message about Christ rather than resting on an assumed national consensus about Christian traditions. As his biographer would later put it:

> In the wake of John Paul's death, the challenge for Polish Catholicism was to look forward, not back; to grapple with and absorb the Magisterium of John Paul II, as well as bask in the spiritual glow of his Polishness and his sanctity; and to find a public voice that mirrored the late Pope's ability to engage society and culture through the arts of reason and persuasion.[4]

Polish Catholics looking ahead will find much to inspire them in the example of John Paul's own life: the Poland in which he grew up was not the one he would know as a young priest or as Archbishop, and things were utterly different again by the time he was old. But he believed that there were bright and strong threads of faith running through Polish—and European—life that could be woven again and again into man's journey through history.

Notes

1   N. Ascherson, *Interview on Pope John Paul II: The Millennial Pope* as found on http://www.pbs.org/wgbh/pages/frontline/shows/pope/interviews/ascherson.html.

2   For a fuller account of this, see J. and J. Bogle, *A Heart for Europe* (Leominster: Gracewing, 1992).

3   See W. Chrostowski, 'The Suffering, Choseness and Mission of the Polish Nation', in *Religion in Eastern Europe* OPREE, Vol. X, Nos. 3 and 6.

4   G. Weigel, *The End and the Beginning* (New York and London: Doubleday, 2010), p. 488.

6

'ALL CHILDREN OF GOD'
JOHN PAUL AND OTHER RELIGIONS

 N OUR TIME, when day by day mankind is being drawn closer together, and the ties between different peoples are becoming stronger, the Church examines more closely her relationship to non-Christian religions. In her task of promoting unity and love among men, indeed among nations, she considers above all in this declaration what men have in common and what draws them to fellowship.[1]

The Second Vatican Council's document *Nostra Aetate* opened the door to a great range of new initiatives in the life of the Catholic Church. In its second paragraph it speaks almost lyrically about man and God:

> One is the community of all peoples, one their origin, for God made the whole human race to live over the face of the earth. One also is their final goal, God. His providence, His manifestations of goodness, His saving design extend to all men until that time when the elect will be united in the Holy City, the city ablaze with the glory of God, where the nations will walk in His light.[2]

The document speaks respectfully of Hinduism and Buddhism, and emphasises that

> The Catholic Church rejects nothing that is true and holy in these religions. She regards with sincere reverence those ways of conduct and of life, those precepts and teachings which, though

differing in many aspects from the ones she holds and sets forth, nonetheless often reflect a ray of that Truth which enlightens all men.[3]

The Moslems, who 'adore the one God, living and subsisting in himself, merciful and all-powerful...' also receive respectful and generous mention.[4]

Special attention is also paid in the document to the Jewish people, speaking of the patriarchs and the prophets and all that binds the Church to the heritage of the Old Testament:

> Since the spiritual patrimony common to Christians and Jews is thus so great, this sacred synod wants to foster and recommend that mutual understanding and respect which is the fruit, above all, of biblical and theological studies as well as of fraternal dialogues.[5]

Nostra Aetate speaks with frankness about the Jews and Christ, but emphasises above all 'the bond that ties the people of the New Covenant to Abraham's stock' and also teaches that

> in her rejection of every persecution against any man, the Church, mindful of the patrimony she shares with the Jews and moved not by political reasons but by the Gospel's spiritual love, decries hatred, persecutions, displays of anti-Semitism, directed against Jews at any time and by anyone.[6]

John Paul would make all of this his own, and dialogue across faith boundaries would be one of the great marks of his pontificate. He made history and opened door after door: the first Pope since St Peter to enter a synagogue, he was also the first ever to bring together the leaders of all the world's main faiths together in one place, that each might pray for peace. And these were not mere one-time gestures but deep-rooted actions that would prove to be of lasting importance and be repeated by his successors, so that it now seems entirely right and normal for a Pope to meet regularly with Jews, for representatives of all faiths to send and receive greetings on various festival days, and for the Pope to be seen as a figure representing mankind's search for goodwill and unity at a spiritual level.

When John Paul spoke at the Synagogue in Rome, he was welcomed by the Rabbi, Dr Elio Toaff, and both read aloud from the Psalms and were seated on identical ceremonial chairs. The Pope was treated with great honour and respect, and the mood was open, genial and friendly. The Rabbi noted that groundwork for the visit had in a sense been laid several years earlier, when Pope John XXIII stopped his car by the synagogue one day in order to bless the people attending a service there.

Now, some twenty years later, standing before a congregation of 1,000, John Paul emphasised that he was building on this and giving thanks for the 'mystery of providence' that had ensured this new goodwill 'between the Jewish community that has been living in this city since the times of the ancient Romans and the Bishop of Rome and universal Pastor of the Catholic Church'.

He then went on to speak, carefully and from the heart. The history of Jews and Christians in the city of Rome was not an easy one: for many years Jews were confined to a ghetto, restricted in employment, banned from sharing in wider community life. John Paul did not shrink from discussing this:

Certainly we cannot and should not forget that the historical circumstances of the past were very different from those that have laboriously matured over the centuries. The general acceptance of a legitimate plurality on the social, civil and religious levels has been arrived at with great difficulty. Nevertheless, a consideration of centuries-long cultural conditioning could not prevent us from recognizing that the acts of discrimination, unjustified limitation of religion freedom, oppression also on the level of civil freedom in regard to the Jews were, from an objective point of view, gravely deplorable manifestations. Yes, once again, through myself, the Church, in the words of the well-known Declaration *Nostra Aetate* deplores the hatred, persecutions and displays of anti Semitism directed against the Jews at any time and by anyone; I repeat: 'by anyone.'[7]

John Paul—too often portrayed as being locked into a box of tradition and restricted by his own roots from seeing a wider picture—was here doing something that could only be done by a man who was prepared to recognise great moral and human truths and give voice to them.

There was also a deep theological understanding that lay behind John Paul's outreach to Jews. In this, as in much else, he turned for assistance to his principle adviser, Cardinal Joseph Ratzinger. Both had played major roles at the Second Vatican Council, and both recognised that it was important to stress that the Church must emphasise that no Christian could claim that the Jewish people, as a race, were responsible for the death of Christ on the Cross—a claim that had been made by Christians in the past and had become rooted in some Catholic folklore. Both sought to express the fullness of the Church's teaching about the Jewish people, and to pay them due tribute as 'the first to hear the Word of God'.[8] Later, Cardinal Ratzinger, as Benedict XVI, would visit not only the Rome synagogue but also the synagogue in Cologne in his native Germany, in the same spirit and with similar warmth and friendship.

Part of John Paul's understanding of the need for the Church to take a fresh approach to the Jews came from his own personal experiences in Poland. Wadowice had a thriving Jewish community and the young Karol's close friend at school, Jerzy Kluger, was Jewish. Their providential reunion in the 1960s was an extraordinary chapter in the drama of both their lives.

Karol, 'Lolek' Wojtyła and Jerzy 'Jurek' Kluger were schoolmates in Wadowice, where Jerzy's father was president of the Jewish community. The two boys played together, skied together, studied together, and spent much time in one another's homes. Both enjoyed learning from Karol's father the stories of Poland's heroes and kings. After school, both planned further studies. The war intervened: Jerzy was among the great numbers of Poles deported to Russia, and after a long series of adventures was finally able to join the Polish Army and fought with distinction at Monte Cassino.

Some twenty years later Jerzy Kluger, working in Rome, heard the name of Karol Wojtyła on the radio where a programme was discussing the arrival of bishops from all over the world for the great Vatican Council. He made enquiries—and the two friends met again. They both had much to tell. Kluger's sister Tesia and his mother and grandmother had all perished in the Holocaust, killed in the gas chambers in Auschwitz.

His father had died in Russia. Alone, after the war, he had gone to Britain where he studied engineering, married, and later brought his wife and family to Italy. They walked and talked for a long time. And when they next met, 'Lolek'—as Jerzy Kluger always still called him, at the former's own request - had arranged for something precious to be sent from Poland –a prayer book belonging to Kluger, which his mother had given to a neighbour when the arrests of Jews began, asking that, if at all possible, it should be given to her son. The neighbour was a friend of Archbishop Wojtyła:

> Lolek had told Mrs Szczepanska that he had found Jurek safe and sound in Rome. Finally she could keep the promise she had made so long ago. She had entrusted the book to Lolek, asking him to give it to me. And now I was holding tightly in my hands the valuable gift, the last that my mother had given me.[9]

Kluger and Wojtyła stayed in contact throughout the 1970s, and in 1978 Kluger, still living in Rome, was at a dentist's office when a nurse announced that a new Pope had been elected, and turned up the radio so that everyone could hear. People were puzzled by the new Pope's accent as he started to speak—he was clearly not Italian—but Kluger knew at once: it was his old friend.

The Kluger family were the first to receive a private audience with Pope John Paul in October 1978. Over the years, there would be many shared meals in the Papal apartment, and Pope John Paul officiated at the wedding of one of Kluger's granddaughters.

All this meant that John Paul's friendship with Jewish people was personal—they had never been an 'other' as they were to many leading churchmen, who had never met or forged friendships with Jews early in their lives.

But there were deeper and more theological reasons for John Paul's sense of urgency in establishing links — reasons connected with teaching the importance of God's covenant, of his faithfulness to his promises, and of the need for all men and women to come to know and trust in God's love.

In John Paul's pontificate, official relations were established between the Holy See and the State of Israel, something which many had thought would be impossible to achieve.

John Paul was also the first Pope ever to visit a mosque—in Damascus in 2001, where he removed his shoes as custom demanded, and shuffled forward—he was by now an old and frail man, and walking with difficulty - and later he spoke to the local people, greeting them with 'May God be with you' in their own language and speaking about peace, and about how Christians and Moslems should work together to teach children about understanding and respect, because violence destroys the image of the Creator in his creatures.

Jerzy Kluger would recall that John Paul more than once said to him 'Jews, Muslims and Christians all believe in the one God' and had added 'These religions have the duty to respect one another, not to make war, and to proclaim to the world that there is only one God!'[10]

One of the most powerful pictures of John Paul as an old man was taken in Jerusalem, where he stood praying at the Western Wall, and inserted a written prayer there, as is the custom:

> God of our fathers, you chose Abraham and his
> descendants to bring your name to the nations. We

*are deeply saddened by the behaviour of those who
in the course of history have caused these children
of yours to suffer and, asking your forgiveness, we
wish to commit ourselves to genuine brotherhood
with the people of the Covenant. Jerusalem 26 March
2000. Joannes Paulus II.*

John Paul's approach to the other religions of the
world—Buddhism, Hinduism, and of course Islam—
was discussed at some length in his book *Crossing the
Threshold of Hope*. This book was a first for any Pope—a
personal response to questions posed by a journalist. It
made headlines when it was published, and indeed the
very idea of such a book seemed astonishing at the time.

On Buddhism, John Paul spoke with careful respect,
quoting *Nostra Aetate*, noting that he had met the Dalai
Lama, and affirming the common quest for peace at
the great Assisi gathering. But he was clear that the
Buddhist idea of 'enlightenment' was deeply at vari-
ance with the Christian tradition of mysticism. In
Buddhism the aim was detachment from the world
and 'The fullness of such detachment is not union with
God but what is called nirvana, a state of perfect
indifference with regard to the world. To save oneself
means, above all, to free oneself from evil by becoming
indifferent to the world, which is the source of evil.' [11]
In contrast, 'Christian mysticism is born of the *Revelation of the Living God*. This God opens Himself to union
with Him, especially by means of the theological
virtues—faith, hope and, above all, love.' [12]

On Hinduism, John Paul noted the insights of
Mahatma Gandhi, who was disillusioned with Christianity which he saw as having been imposed by colonial
powers. The Second Vatican Council, recognising this
problem, sought to take a fresh approach, emphasising

that the Church recognises that Hindus seek to explore the divine mystery and to express it through myths and through philosophical insight. Commenting on this John Paul reminisced about the great Assisi meeting, noting the 'number of common elements' found in the great variety of religions in the world.

John Paul's meetings with Moslems were of importance to him. He noted with respect their 'fidelity to prayer' which, he said, was a model for some Christians who 'having deserted their magnificent cathedrals, pray only a little or not at all.'[13] His meeting with young Moslems in Casablanca was 'unforgettable', and they were open to him when he spoke about faith in the one God.[14] But there are problems with the Koran:

> In Islam all the richness of God's self-revelation, which constitutes the heritage of the Old and New Testaments, has definitely been set aside. Some of the most beautiful names in the human language are given to the God of the Koran, but He is ultimately a God outside of the world, a God who is only Majesty, never Emmanuel, God-with-us. Islam is not a religion of redemption.[15]

Throughout his pontificate, John Paul sought dialogue, mutual respect, and a sharing in common values with the other religions of the world. He remained serenely convinced of the spread of the Gospel of Christ, seeing in every man the need to search for something great beyond himself:

> This is the most profound truth about man. Christ is the first to know this truth. He truly knows 'that which is in every man'... With His Gospel He has touched the intimate truth of man. He has touched it with His Cross.[16]

Notes

1   Vatican II, *Nostra Aetate*, 1.
2   *Ibid.*
3   *Ibid.*, 2.
4   Cf. *ibid.*, 3.
5   *Ibid.*, 4.
6   *Ibid.*
7   Pope John Paul II, Address at the Synagogue of Rome (13 April 1986). See also *Nostra Aetate*, 4.
8   *Roman Missal*, prayers for Good Friday.
9   J. Kluger, *The Pope and I* (New York: Orbis Books 2012), p. 77.
10 *Ibid.*, p. 222.
11 John Paul II, *Crossing the Threshold of Hope* (London: Jonathan Cape 1994), p. 86.
12 *Ibid.*, p. 88.
13 *Ibid.*, p. 93.
14 *Ibid.*, p. 94.
15 *Ibid.*, p. 92.
16 *Ibid.*, p. 104.

7

FREEDOM

OR YOUNG POLES in the 1940s, 'freedom' was a watchword that had a specific meaning, associated with freedom from foreign oppression—whether from Germany in the West or Russia in the East—and from political oppression, from the Nazis or the Communists. It meant freedom to be Polish, to earn a living and raise a family in peace, to talk and study freely without fear of arrest, freedom to write and publish books and poetry, plays and songs, in one's own language and expressing a range of political and religious views. It did not necessarily mean freedom to do whatever one wanted: life was tough and all sorts of things were in any case at that stage impossible (travelling the world with a backpack and a mobile telephone, for example). And it was not fully defined—it simply expressed the longing of an oppressed people to live in peace and dignity, as human beings with rights, free to do great things and ordinary things.

It was in this environment that Karol Wojtyła pondered the meaning of 'freedom'. And, later, as a priest and bishop under Communism, sharing the treasures of the Christian faith with people in all sorts of conditions, he thought and taught much about the subject. What is freedom, really? What does it means to be 'free'? Why has God placed in our hearts this desire for a sense of freedom, and how is it connected with our joy, our sense of being fully alive?

In the 1960s and 70s, in the West, 'freedom' came to mean a whole range of things that young Poles in the 1940s would not have recognised as linked to their longing for freedom. The word 'freedom' came to mean the right to use drugs such as cocaine or heroin, the right to abort a baby, the right to have a number of sexual partners. Responding to this, some in the Church struggled to find ways to discuss freedom, and it was tempting to abandon the attempt, and to talk instead about obeying rules, or adhering to traditions, in order to shore up the Church's message. Karol Wojtyła found another way to approach the subject.

Freedom, for Karol Wojtyła/John Paul II, was always linked to truth. Freedom must be grounded in truth, if it is to have any real meaning and not to dwindle into new forms of servitude.

The truth about man, his relationship to God, his relationship to other people, includes a full recognition of his freedom: freedom to choose between good and evil, between things that are trite and superficial and things that have real meaning, between truth and falsehood. The first freedom is freedom of religion.

Truth cannot be imposed—it 'imposes itself' by the strength of its own reality. For this reason, it cannot really be imposed by a government—not even by one seeking to do so with the best of intentions. Thus the Church need not fear religious pluralism as such, because such pluralism does not necessarily lead to indifference—on the contrary, given freedom to operate, the Church will flourish, because of its truth, which will always and everywhere find a response, and a great one.

This was the thinking that Archbishop Wojtyła brought to the Second Vatican Council in the 1960s, and shared with other Council Fathers. The debate on religious freedom would prove to be one of the most contentious of the Council, but also one of the most fruitful.

Archbishop Wojtyła brought to the Council an understanding of what it was like living under a repressive government: random arrests of clergy and active lay apostles, restrictions on church publications and use of the media, the banning of Church activity in public spaces and enforcement of rules confining all prayer to church buildings, and so forth.

Archbishop Wojtyła asked important questions. He spoke for the 'Church of Silence', crushed and burdened by the cruelties of an atheist regime. The men and women living—and suffering for—their Faith in this way had something to bring to the Church meeting in Council in Rome, raising questions that had in fact been simmering for a long while. What sort of freedom does the Church seek, and why? Why had the Marxist atheist idea proved attractive to some serious thinkers, given its contradictions and its crude attempts to reinvent human nature? What did the Church's own history have to say about freedom? And, crucially: could the Church could with integrity, claim the right to real freedom of action if it sought to restrict the freedom of non-believers?

The persecution of the Church in the twentieth century—the most savage and wide-ranging in the Church's long history, and producing more martyrs than ever before—would one day result in a great flowering of the Christian faith: of this Karol Wojtyła had no doubt. He did not believe—as many did, who were suffering under Communism—that the Marxist tyranny would endure for long years to come. He believed that it held within it the seeds of its own decay. But what would come next? What should the Church be saying to future generations? What would the martyrs of the twentieth century bequeath to the Church of all time? What about the question of religious freedom?

The Second Vatican Council, profoundly influenced by the contribution of the Archbishop of Krakow among others, examined the whole question of religious freedom in great depth. It was a subject that had not been adequately explored in its modern setting. For long years the phrase 'religious freedom' had been used by opponents of the Church to attack or undermine her mission. But the Church now wanted to speak out on this subject. The Church upheld truth, and sought to teach truth: but did this mean that the Church did not really believe in human freedom, in the free use of the mind to explore truth? Did it mean that the Catholic Faith should be imposed by force of law, and if so, how?

George Weigel notes:

> At the time Wojtyła entered the religious freedom debate, the argument was stalled at the level of Church-state theory—between proponents who were primarily interested in disentangling the Church from altar-and- throne arrangements, and opponents who were convinced that religious freedom was the opening wedge to religious indifferentism and subsequent governmental hostility. By putting the question in a personalist context and showing how the transcendence of the human person, manifested in freedom 'faces' towards God, the archbishop of Krakow demonstrated that religious freedom could be vigorously defended without reducing 'freedom' to a matter of indifference between opinions.[1]

The resulting document *Dignitatis Humanae* (1965) emphasised religious freedom as the will of God, as something linked to the Church's understanding of the dignity of man and his ability to seek and find truth:

> This Vatican Council likewise professes its belief that it is upon the human conscience that these obligations fall and exert their binding force. The truth cannot impose itself except by virtue of its own truth, as it makes its entrance into the mind at once quietly and with power.[2]

Thus, to assert the primacy of Christ over all things—a central tenet of the Christian understanding of creation and redemption—does not necessarily bind the Church to a particular form of government. *Dignitatis Humanae* thus goes beyond the discussion about 'separation of Church and State' which had been an issue since the French Revolution of the eighteenth century. The Council Fathers effectively affirmed that speaking of such separation missed the point because what matters is truth, and man's duty to seek it.

The Church cannot, in any real sense, be separated from anything—one cannot speak of a separation between the Church and the arts, or the Church and sport, or the Church and science. But in order to ensure that the Church can bring Christ into everything, it is not necessary to establish a set structure in which this is done: the Church can find a whole range of ways. And religious pluralism does not mean that government should remain indifferent to the Church or unable to assist and promote her work. Religious freedom, properly understood, affirms human dignity rooted in truth: humans have a desire for God and will seek him. Thus, in the words of *Dignitatis Humanae*:

> Government therefore ought indeed to take
> account of the religious life of the citizenry and
> show it favour, since the function of govern-
> ment is to make provision for the common
> welfare. However, it would clearly transgress
> the limits set to its power, were it to presume
> to command or inhibit acts that are religious.[3]

Moreover when John Paul II became Pope, it was this
freedom that he sought to explore. At the heart of John
Paul's understanding of freedom was an understanding of the importance of the human person. When he
returned to Poland after his election as Pope, in words
that were to resonate across the country with powerful
long-term results, he said:

> ... man cannot be fully understood without
> Christ. Or rather, man is incapable of under-
> standing himself fully without Christ. He
> cannot understand who he is, nor what his true
> dignity is, nor what his vocation is, nor what
> his final end is. He cannot understand any of
> this without Christ. Therefore Christ cannot be
> kept out of the history of man in any part of the
> globe, at any longitude or latitude of geogra-
> phy. The exclusion of Christ from the history of
> man is an act against man.[4]

Those who were present at the great events of the 1979
pilgrimage sensed that they were sharing in something
much greater than the mere celebration of a Polish
Pope and the realisation that the iron grip of the
Communist regime must inevitably bend to this reality. 'It was much, much more than that' one participant
recalls. 'We all felt that things would no longer be the
same. To be honest, I felt as if some sort of miracle had
occurred. And people became different—they started

to behave differently. This was not a political thing—it was somehow something supernatural.'[5]

John Paul did not refer to Communism in his homilies: he did not speak of political matters at all. He spoke instead about man and God, about the innate dignity that every human being has, by virtue of being human and created by God, and his message was a timeless one which spoke to the deepest needs of the human heart.

This was the message that John Paul would preach to the world. It would prove immensely attractive, not only to his countrymen, who would in due course throw off the yoke of Communism and win back their own freedom as a nation, but also to a worldwide audience.

His first encyclical *Redemptor Hominis* (1979) tackled the subject. Quoting the words of Christ: 'You will know the truth, and the truth will make you free', John Paul emphasised that Christ calls man to 'an honest relationship with regard to truth as a condition for authentic freedom.' To be truly free, it is necessary to avoid 'every kind of illusory freedom, every superficial unilateral freedom, every freedom that fails to enter into the whole truth about man and the world.'[6]

Later, in *Centesimus Annus*, he emphasised that the link between truth and freedom also had political implications. A society could not be free if it abandoned the notion of truth. The idea that there is no truth, that there are no moral absolutes, renders the normal functioning of a free society impossible.

> If there is no ultimate truth to guide and direct political activity, then ideas and convictions can easily be manipulated for reasons of power ... In a world without truth, freedom loses its founda-

tion and man is exposed to the violence of passion
and to manipulation, both open and hidden.[7]

Centesimus Annus (1991) was published to mark the
centenary of Leo XIII's great encyclical on social justice,
Rerum Novarum. It marked the opening of a new era
in the Church, with a recognition of changing times,
industrialisation, democracy, and the new societies
that were emerging in the nineteenth century.

A century after Leo, John Paul enunciated the
Church's position:

> The Church values the democratic system
> inasmuch as it ensures the participation of
> citizens in making political choices, guarantees
> to the governed the possibility both of electing
> and holding accountable those who govern
> them, and of replacing them through peaceful
> means when appropriate. Thus she cannot
> encourage the formation of narrow ruling
> groups which usurp the power of the State for
> individual interests or for ideological ends.

Furthermore

> Following the collapse of Communist totalitari-
> anism and of many other totalitarian and
> 'national security' regimes, today we are witness-
> ing a predominance, not without signs of oppo-
> sition, of the democratic ideal, together with
> lively attention to and concern for human rights.
> But for this very reason it is necessary for peoples
> in the process of reforming their systems to give
> democracy an authentic and solid foundation
> through the explicit recognition of those rights.
> Among the most important of these rights,
> mention must be made of the right to life, an
> integral part of which is the right of the child to

develop in the mother's womb from the moment of conception; the right to live in a united family and in a moral environment conducive to the growth of the child's personality; the right to develop one's intelligence and freedom in seeking and knowing the truth; the right to share in the work which makes wise use of the earth's material resources, and to derive from that work the means to support oneself and one's dependents; and the right freely to establish a family, to have and to rear children through the responsible exercise of one's sexuality. In a certain sense, the source and synthesis of these rights is religious freedom, understood as the right to live in the truth of one's faith and in conformity with one's transcendent dignity as a person.[8]

John Paul had witnessed the errors of the twentieth century at first hand, and the call for human beings to seek a better future came from the heart of the Church and was frank. Slick calls for democracy and freedom would be of no avail unless there was a reality based on truth: 'As history demonstrates, a democracy without values easily turns into open or thinly disguised totalitarianism.'[9]

And a few years later, in 1995, he was speaking in detail about specific instances where the loss of values was already threatening freedom—with the 'eclipse of the value of life',[10] abortifacient drugs, euthanasia, and the destruction of human embryos following in-vitro fertilisation. In *Evangelium Vitae* (1995) he warned that in society where even infanticide is accepted, reverts to 'a state of barbarism which one hoped had been left behind forever.'[11] Killing the weak and vulnerable instead of caring for them is 'the death of true freedom'.[12]

For John Paul, the dignity of every human being was at the core of discussions about freedom and about political choices. The protection of human life—in the womb, in a hospital bed, in places where humans were in need—was central to human freedom. The word 'freedom' was not a convenient label under which selfishness and cruelty could be honoured. Freedom must be anchored in truth, including the truth about human beings.

John Paul's passionate commitment to freedom and truth brought him headlines and dramatic debates in the media: when *Veritatis Splendor* was published in 1993, it received massive worldwide coverage and politicians, women's groups, academics, lobby groups and self-styled celebrities were giving their opinions on it as the major topic of news, in a way that would have seemed quite unimaginable with the publication of an encyclical in, say, the 1920s and 30s.

This was partly because media attention focused on the encyclical's clear statements with regard to sexual morality. But there was also a sort of shock that anyone would dare to make the link between the abandonment of moral values and the loss of freedom. John Paul's message was serious:

> Today, when many countries have seen the fall of ideologies which bound politics to a totalitarian conception of the world—Marxism being the foremost of these—there is no less grave a danger that the fundamental rights of the human person will be denied and that the religious yearnings which arise in the heart of every human being will be absorbed once again into politics. This is *the risk of an alliance between democracy and ethical relativism,* which would remove any sure moral reference point from political and social life, and

on a deeper level make the acknowledgement of truth impossible.[13]

Many (perhaps most?) of the people who commented on the encyclical—whether on TV or in the local pub—had not read it, and relied on media reports. But one message that was widely absorbed was that the Pope was a man of strong and deeply held moral convictions whose understanding of major issues had not been formed by merely reading a book of rules and then repeating them. And, for those who took even a short time to reflect before voicing an opinion about him also recognised that this was the man who had played a major role—perhaps the major role—in the collapse of Communism. It was not easy simply to dismiss him as a bigot who sought to impose an arbitrary set of rules on the world. He spoke the language of human rights. His message was not one of announcing rules but of calling for human dignity to be respected. Moral values matter because

> in every sphere of personal, family, social and political life, morality—founded upon truth and open in truth to authentic freedom—renders a primordial, indispensable and immensely valuable service not only for the individual person and his growth in the good, but also for society and its genuine development.[14]

An understanding of human freedom was central to John Paul's thinking, to his teaching, to the way he lived and worked. The value of every human life, the sanctuary of the family as the place where human beings were to be cherished and receive care, the need for human beings to recognise each other's needs and work together as a community for the good of all—

these things were bound up with freedom and could not be sliced away from it. 'Freedom' was not a word synonymous with selfishness, or with buying consumer goods. Freedom is not slogans about holidays. Freedom is not bullying others into agreeing about your version of freedom. Freedom is anchored in truth—the truth about human beings, their value, their irreplaceable importance, their rights—beginning with the right to life itself. John Paul taught repeatedly about freedom and its importance not because he had been forced to live under regimes which denied freedom, but because he recognised that freedom is threatened by a refusal to recognise the moral norms which alone allow it to exist and flourish. This message is not new, but he gave it a fresh impetus and urgency as he led the Church into a new millennium, in which freedom's vulnerability seemed uncomfortably clear.

Notes

[1]   G. Weigel, *Witness to Hope* (New York and London: Harper-Collins, 1999), p. 164.

[2]   Vatican II, *Dignitatis Humanae*, 1.

[3]   *Ibid.*, 3.

[4]   John Paul II, *Speech in Victory Square Warsaw* (2 June 1979).

[5]   P. Kloczowski, conversation with the authors, 2013.

[6]   John Paul II, *Redemptor Hominis*, 12

[7]   John Paul II *Centesimus Annus*, 46.

[8]   *Ibid.*

[9]   *Ibid.*

[10]   John Paul II, *Evangelium Vitae*, 10.

[11]   *Ibid.*,14.

[12]   *Ibid.*,20.

[13]   John Paul II, *Veritatis Splendor*, 101.

[14]   *Ibid.*

8

A SPECIAL GRACE OF PRAYER

VERY TIME AND every place is a time and a place for prayer' — this saying from St Catherine of Siena is completely personified by the life of Karol Wojtyła . It was said of him that he did not pray the same way as he breathed, but he breathed the same way as he prayed. In this way, prayer became the rhythm of his heart and was the fulcrum of each day.

From earliest childhood, formal prayer had a great importance in his life: the Mass, the Angelus, the rosary and the Stations of the Cross. Even as Pope he made a daily habit of saying the Prayer to the Holy Spirit and making the consecration to the Sacred Heart. As all priests are required to do, he said the Breviary, the Divine Office, which gives a rhythm to the day via a selection of psalms and Scripture readings to be recited at certain times. If he was travelling or otherwise busy, the Holy Father would never neglect this duty, but fit it in as best he could. He could pray it in a kayak or an aeroplane and be perfectly recollected. This ability to pray at 'every time and place' was the fruit of a lifetime dedicated to spending time in prayer every day.

Prayer is something God does in us — the deeper we go into prayer, the more it becomes the action of God. Prayer in the early stages is our reaching out to God, although it is always in response to grace working within us. St Teresa of Avila makes a distinction between active prayer ('saying one's prayers') which comes from the effort of the person praying and the prayer of quiet, which is a pure gift of God in which the mind and faculties are stilled and focused on God.

It must be said at once that mystical prayer is a gift of God and that while many holy people have attained it, it is not a requirement for holiness. John Paul's advice to others is simple:

> Pray any way you like, so long as you do pray. You can pray the way your mother taught you, you can use a prayer book. Sometimes it takes courage to pray, but it is possible to pray and necessary to pray. Whether from memory or a book or just in thought, it is all the same.[1]

When he met Tyranowski, the young Wojtyła may have been experiencing the first stirrings of the prayer of quiet, which can begin almost imperceptibly in one who has the discipline and habit of regular prayer. Tyranowski, a gifted spiritual guide, would have been able to help the young student develop his interior life. Outwardly, there was almost certainly no sign of any of this—Karol was known to be devout—among his friends he appeared as he always was.

By the time he discerned his vocation, Wojtyła had enough understanding to realise that he was called to be contemplative in the way described by Teresa of Avila and John of the Cross, to 'pray without ceasing' (1 Th 5:17). At first he believed that this could only mean a monastic vocation as a Carmelite, but his superiors thought differently. In that case, the young priest would have to become a contemplative as a busy diocesan priest, which would not be easy. Tyranowski managed it in the lay state while holding down a job and caring for his mother, so perhaps this was the will of God for him?

From praying with words to resting wordlessly before God, formal prayer became a springboard into contemplation. As a young priest, hiking in the mountains with his students, saying Mass in the open air, camping and kayaking, Wojtyła only had to open his breviary for everyone to know that *Wujek* ('Uncle') needed to be alone. He wouldn't just read it through but pause to savour each word, spending longer on his reading than would normally be the case. There is a monastic tradition of *lectio divina* where Scripture is meditated on deeply in short passages and this is probably what was happening here. Sometimes while out hiking, the young priest's eyes would suddenly unfocus as if he were withdrawing into himself—this too became a sign that he needed time alone.

Wojtyła remained devoted to the traditional prayers of his youth and never abandoned them. He prayed the Stations of the Cross and the Angelus in much the same way as his breviary—rather than mechanically reciting, he would make frequent pauses in deep meditation as if drawing strength from every word. People close to the Holy Father believed that he had received a special grace of prayer that enabled him to enter into human existence at a deeper level. This grace was what sustained him during the long years of service to the Church and the suffering that he underwent. Even as he grew older, he had an apparently boundless energy, exhausting those of his household who accompanied him, yet he worked longer hours than anyone.

Cardinal Angelo Scola has described what it was like to pray alongside the Holy Father:

> When we went to lunch with him, we went first to the chapel to say the Angelus. All of us thought that it would take about thirty seconds. Instead sometimes it took so long that we could no longer remain on our knees on the floor. The

> Pope was truly immersed in prayer and for him
> space and time no longer existed ... In his
> prayers I perceived, I could see, a profound
> dialogue with God.[2]

When immersed in prayer, the Holy Father lost all sense
of his surroundings and also of time. His aides often
had to tap him gently to prevent him from missing
engagements. In making arrangements for his travel,
his household would suggest to his hosts that any route
taken by the Holy Father should avoid passing a chapel
where the Eucharist was reserved, because John Paul
could never pass the Blessed Sacrament without
pausing in prayer, usually for long periods.

There is no doubt that he was a mystic and it seems
that he was often overcome by an inner compulsion to
pray, following Jesus' invitation to his disciples to 'come
away and rest for a while' (Mk 6:31). When responding
to this deep interior urge—indeed, longing—he would
claim 'tiredness' or some such excuse, only to be found
later in the chapel, transfixed in prayer. People also
found him deep at prayer in a bathroom, kneeling next
to the sink, and on one occasion a broom cupboard. Yet
this grace, one might call it a 'charism', did not make
him aloof from the rest of humanity but drew him
closer. His ability to focus on every person he met,
making them feel as if they were the only person in the
room, was a fruit of this prayer.

One example among many comes from an American prison psychologist who was able to attend one of
the Pope's private masses with her mother.

> When we stood in the reception room afterward
> he made the rounds as always, and when he
> reached us his secretary whispered in his ear, I
> suppose telling him to switch to English; then

> he looked at us for a moment and said in his
> profound, drawn-out, leonine rumble: 'Mother
> and daughter' accompanied by a look of love.
> I have lived in that love ever since. Seriously, I
> have evoked that memory when the prisoners
> insult me or when the bosses question my
> judgment or when I am in dread of the future.[3]

The Holy Father always prepared very carefully before
Mass, ensuring that he was in a state of recollection,
and never failed to make his thanksgiving after Mass
which priests were required to do. Today with the
increasing demands of modern life this is a practice
that is diminishing, but the Pope was never too busy
to make time for God.

Many witnesses speak of the strange sounds that
the Pope would make during prayer, as if he were
bringing all the pains of the world to God. In the words
of Scripture: 'the Spirit helps us in our weakness. For
we do not know what to pray for as we ought, but the
Spirit himself intercedes for us with groanings too
deep for words' (Rm 8:26). The American doctor
quoted above describes being in the Pope's private
chapel before his Mass:

> Those noises are among my strongest memo-
> ries. The first time I went I couldn't understand
> where the lion-like, almost roaring sounds were
> coming from and then I saw the Pope at the
> prie-dieu. I had not even noticed he was in the
> chapel. It was mesmerizing. What is the verse
> about praying with groanings that cannot be
> uttered? That is what it was.

These inarticulate noises may not always have
sounded the same. In interview already mentioned,

Cardinal Scola spoke of 'sounds like the gurgles of a river without end'.

If the Holy Father at prayer, oblivious to time and those around him, was in danger of throwing awry his daily timetable it was not from bad time management or insensitivity to the needs of others. For Karol Wojtyła, God came first. When problems arose, he would say 'Let's pray about it some more and then decide'. He prayed before appointing new bishops, and he prayed before making every important decision, even if it meant delay.

God declares through the psalmist 'be still and know that I am God' (Ps 46:10); Pope John Paul II made these words his own by attaining that stillness which transcends the preoccupations of daily life and draws the soul into a condition of total absorption in God, so that all the other faculties seem to be asleep.

> In vain is your earlier rising,
> your going later to rest,
> you who toil for the bread you eat;
> when he pours gifts on his beloved
> while they slumber. (Ps 127, Grail version)

What were John Paul's spiritual practices?

Karol Wojtyła prayed with his body as well as his mind. As a child, he saw his father kneeling to pray, and this habit remained with him until the very end of his life when he was wheelchair-bound and unable to stand. During a Corpus Christi procession in 2004, when travelling by Popemobile with a monstrance in front of him, the ailing Pope begged to be allowed to kneel. The road was not very even, so it was suggested he wait awhile. Eventually, the Holy Father became visibly agitated 'but Jesus is here! I want to kneel!' and so two assistants helped him out of his chair and onto the prie-dieu. It was obvious at once that he could not kneel independently and so after a few moments, the Holy Father was placed back in his chair. When at prayer, the Holy Father would often bury his face in his hands. This became the most common sight of him at prayer, as if he was raising a great weight of problems to the Lord. If he were saying the rosary, he would rest his head on one hand and count the beads with the other.

Alone in his chapel, Karol Wojtyła would often prostrate himself on the ground, his arms wide, in a cruciform position. This must have been a long-term practice. As a young man praying that the Nazis would not find him during their sweep of Krakow after the Warsaw uprising of 1944, Karol prostrated himself on the basement floor while the soldiers' boots rang on the stone steps outside. As a bishop with many concerns on his mind, he would spend whole nights on the stone floor in prayer. It was not unknown for a sacristan entering the chapel in the morning to find him asleep in this way.

His devotion to the rosary was legendary and, like Padre Pio, he was seldom seen without one. He saw the rosary as a genuine training in holiness, each time the mysteries of Christ's life and death unfold and are contemplated. His Apostolic Letter of 2002, *Rosarium Virginis Mariae* explains this further:

> Listening and meditation are nourished by silence. After the announcement of the mystery and the proclamation of the word, it is fitting to pause and focus one's attention for a suitable period of time on the mystery concerned, before moving into vocal prayer. A discovery of the importance of silence is one of the secrets of

practising contemplation and meditation. One
drawback of a society dominated by technology
and the mass media is the fact that silence
becomes increasingly difficult to achieve.[4]

Allowing silence to grow within is one of the important
stages of developing in the contemplative life.

The importance of *Totus Tuus* in chapter four in the
life of the Pope has been noted; the Holy Father would
often stop by the statue of Our Lady as if deep in
conversation with her. When asked if he had ever had
a vision of her, he replied no, but he had sensed her
presence. His mysticism was not one of locutions,
visions and physical phenomena.

The many reported healings of the sick which began
during his lifetime, were above all an occasion to give
thanks to God. In an interview with the authors,
Cardinal Dziwicz said that the Holy Father never liked
to discuss healings and other miraculous events associated with his intercession, insisting that it is God who
heals. Pope John Paul II prayed for everyone he met.
Thousands of requests for his prayers poured into his
office, his secretaries would write them onto pieces of
paper which the Holy Father took with him before the
Blessed Sacrament. He not only prayed for individuals
but for whole countries.

Despite his early reputation as a reformer, Papa
Wojtyła's spirituality was innately traditional and
Polish. He loved to remember significant dates such as
name days and birthdays. Staff got the day off on the
feast of St Charles Borromeo, his name day. He loved
special occasions such as Christmas, which he celebrated
each year in Polish style, distributing the *oplatek* bread
and singing the traditional hymns, which he knew by
heart. After the assassination attempt, the Holy Father

celebrated Mass at 5 pm every 13 May, in thanksgiving for his life. Only his regular household was invited to this special and very personal remembrance.

As Pope, John Paul II liked to work in his bedroom which was cooler there than in his office, and he preferred an open window for fresh air. The room was simple with just a bed, a wardrobe and chest of drawers. He had few possessions. Above the door was a copy of Brother Albert's painting *Ecce Homo*, and there was also a picture of the Divine Mercy given to him by his great friend Cardinal Deskur, who had introduced the young Wojtyła to the devotion while the two were still seminarians. In his study there was a large picture of Our Lady of, Częstochowa and on his desk a photo of Cardinal Sapieha. There was also a statue of the Immaculate Conception which he would kiss as he passed by.

In his private chapel the Holy Father had several relics that meant a great deal to him: A fragment of the True Cross, relics of St Jadwiga, Queen of Poland, St Stanislaus, patron of Poland, Saints Peter and Paul, Brother Albert, St Faustina and a hair of Maximilian Kolbe. He would regularly kiss these as he passed in his wheelchair. As Pope, he canonised nearly five hundred saints and beatified many more, the 'saint factory' perhaps a means of encouraging the whole Church by example, remembering Tyranowski's exhortation from so long ago that anyone can be a saint, it's not difficult! The Holy Father was also devoted to St Charles Borromeo, his name saint, St Francis of Assisi and St John of the Cross.

Although he encouraged the new movements in the Church, his own spirituality remained as it had always been. He passionately believed in the power of intercessory prayer. Wojtyła did not only have recourse to the saints in heaven, but also to those still alive. One holy man in whom he placed especial trust was Padre Pio. The two first met in the late 1940s when was studying in Rome and decided to travel to southern Italy to meet the famed wonder worker. They spoke at length, though little details exist about what was said. It is said that the young priest asked the stigmatic which of the wounds of Christ was the most painful, and was told the shoulder wound. For many years after St Pio's death, it was not generally known about this particular wound. There has been discussion about whether the Holy Man of the Gargano prophesied that the young Pole would become Pope, and, despite Wojtyła's denials, rumours still remain. In any case, there was a rapport between the two men of God and in 1962, during the Second Vatican Council Bishop Wojtyła wrote to Padre Pio to ask for his prayers for a young mother, dangerously ill with a tumour. At the time Padre Pio was not regarded very favourably in the Vatican, many suspecting he was a fraud. The young woman made a miraculous recovery.

On rising at 5 am, the Holy Father would pray and meditate for two hours before he was ready for Mass which he said at 7 am. On Fridays he would pray the Stations of the Cross, which he liked to do on the Vatican's rooftop garden. At noon he would recite the Angelus and after lunch he would read, sometimes philosophy or theology, but often Polish literature such as the trilogy by Sienkiewicz, which his father had first read to him. He prayed a litany every day, such as the Litany of the Saints, Loreto, the Sacred Heart, the Litany of the Polish Nation. He was especially fond of the Litany of Our Lord Jesus Christ Priest and Victim, which had been recited at the seminary. As well as the Breviary, Pope John Paul II would read a passage of Scripture each day. Tuesdays would be his day off when he would leave Rome for the pleasures of the countryside, perhaps visiting a shrine such as Mentorella. If Wojtyła's life was a synthesis of prayer and action, it was because he drew his seemingly boundless energy and strength from prayer.

> Those who were his confidants noted that John Paul II was well aware that 'the Pope's first responsibility toward the Church and toward the world is to pray' and that 'from prayer he derived the capacity of speaking the truth without fear, since one who is alone before God has no fear of men'.[5]

In recent years ascesis has fallen out of favour, and some of Wojtyła' s penances may seem a little harsh or strange to modern people. For instance, he owned practically nothing and gave away much of his clothing. He refused to wear new things, and when his underwear was falling to bits and beyond repair, his household was reduced to buying new items and buffeting them to make them appear worn. Although a man who enjoyed his food, especially Polish food (his fondness for the Kremowka cream cake is well-known), he was abstemious, especially during Lent when he would eat only one meal. He fasted before ordinations. As a bishop, he had been asked to select a car for himself, which he duly did but when it arrived it seemed more luxurious than he had expected. After a little while, he traded it in for a cheaper vehicle, giving the surplus money to the poor.

The Church has a long tradition of physical penance, although it is not spoken of much today. Very few people knew that Wojtyła practised it; he kept a special belt with which he chastised himself in private. It is not known when this began, but as bishop and Pope he maintained this practice. Mortification of the flesh has included self-flagellation from earliest times; St Francis, St Thomas More, St Pio, Mother Teresa and many others all practised it. There is no intention to cause lasting injury or attain spiritual one-upmanship, but an imitation of St Paul who spoke of chastising his body and bringing it under control (1 Co 9:27). All ascetic disciplines are intended to 'subdue the passions' and are never an end in themselves.

If Papa Wojtyła was a physical and a spiritual athlete, it was not from any desire to impress but a means of complete self-giving to God. In the end, the greatest mystical experiences known to humankind have no meaning if they do not accompany spiritual fruit. It is difficult to know what heights of prayer Wojtyła reached; there are things known only to his confessor and in a way it is not necessary for us to know. The true worth of anyone is in the way they think, speak and act; 'by their fruits you will know them' (Mt 7:16). The life and work of this remarkable Pope continue to bear great fruit.

Notes

1   Pope John Paul II, *The Way of Prayer* (New York: Crossroad 1995), p. 59.
2   Interview with Cardinal Scola, *Corriere della Sera* (7 January 2011). English translation at: angeloscola.it/English.
3   M. Wright, correspondence with C. Anderson, September 2013.
4   Pope John Paul II, *Rosarium Virginis Mariae*, 31.
5   S. Oder, *Why He is a Saint* (USA: Rizzoli International, 2010), p. 147.

9

The Divine Mercy

N THE LIFE of the Church great devotions have always sprung up within a historical context. They bring a much needed message or correction to the time in which they are sent. Thus the devotion to the Sacred Heart appeared in France in the late seventeenth century, a time when the philosophy of Rationalism favoured either atheism or an impersonal God. This message of Christ's burning love for us was also an antidote to the chief heresies of the time: Calvinism and Jansenism (which began in a French convent) which emphasised the anger and punishment of an unforgiving God.

In the twentieth century a prevailing heresy was modernism which although condemned at the beginning of the twentieth century has continued in one guise or another. Like Rationalism, it undermines the miraculous elements in Scripture; for example proposing that Christ didn't know he was divine, that the Resurrection didn't happen. It also teaches that personal sin is of far less consequence than the sins of societies. In parts of the world where terrible injustice occurs, it is easy to see how ideas such as these can take root through years of desperation. At the opposite end of Modernism is a particularly rigorous form of traditionalism which emphasises strict rules and opposes any form of development in doctrine or practice.

John Paul's first encyclical was *Redemptor Hominis* in 1979:

> The Redeemer of Man, Jesus Christ, is the centre
> of the universe and of history. To him go my
> thoughts and my heart in this solemn moment of
> the world that the Church and the whole family
> of present-day humanity are now living ...[1]

The second encyclical was on the subject of Divine
Mercy. This puzzled many commentators, who had
been expecting something which perhaps challenged
Communism—then still the official ideology of the
Pope's native Poland and of the vast and seemingly
extremely powerful Union of Soviet Socialist Republics—or which perhaps rallied Christians to a message
of unity around a Catholic Church which seemed to
be gathering a new sense of confidence following the
confusing years of the immediate post-Vatican II
period.

The message of *Dives in Misericordia* in 1980—'rich
in mercy'—thus perhaps initially seemed rather
obscure. John Paul emphasised, however, that this
second encyclical in a sense flowed on naturally from
the first—and carried a message about modern man
that was urgent and compelling. Christ, he said,
brought to us all the mercy of God, and this was
something of which all were in desperate need:

> The present-day mentality, more perhaps than
> that of people in the past, seems opposed to a
> God of mercy, and in fact tends to exclude from
> life and to remove from the human heart the
> very idea of mercy. The word and the concept
> of "mercy" seem to cause uneasiness in man,
> who, thanks to the enormous development of
> science and technology, never before known in
> history, has become the master of the earth and
> has subdued and dominated it. This dominion
> over the earth, sometimes understood in a

one—sided and superficial way, seems to have
no room for mercy.[2]

In writing about God's mercy, John Paul seemed to be
inspired by two very specific themes. The first of these
was a deep understanding of fatherhood, of what it
means to love as a father, and of God as the 'Father of
mercies'. All of this is illustrated in the encyclical with
a detailed exploration of the father in the story of the
Prodigal Son—a figure of love and strength and
tenderness, who never allows his repentant son to
humiliate himself or to feel less than loved and welcomed in the family home. The second theme was that
of modern man, and the longing to have somewhere
to place to sorrow and the misery, the mistakes and
the hatred and the misplaced zeal that had brought
about the horrors of the twentieth century. These
horrors were all part of the lives and experiences and
memories of people living in 1980: the battlefields of
two world wars with young men being slaughtered
on a massive scale, the horrors of Nazism and Communism, the long-drawn-out suffering of the Gulag,
the seemingly invincible march of totalitarian ideologies. Poland had been very particularly caught up in
this, suffering under both Nazis and Communism.
    As John Paul puts it:

> Those who remember, who were witnesses and
> participants in the events of those years and the
> horrible sufferings they caused for millions of
> people, know well how necessary was the
> message of mercy.[3]

Papal biographer George Weigel notes:

> John Paul II had an acute sense of the gaping
> holes that had been torn in the moral and

spiritual fabric of humanity by the murderous cruelties of the twentieth century. A century that began with a robust human confidence in the future had ended with a thick fog of cynicism hanging over the western world. As he wrote in his striking 2003 apostolic letter, *The Church in Europe*, Christianity's historic heartland (and, by extension, the entire western world) was beset by guilt over what it had done in two world wars and the Cold War, at Auschwitz and in the Gulag, through the Ukrainian hunger famine and the communist persecution of the Church. But having abandoned the God of the Bible, it had nowhere to turn to confess this guilt, seek absolution, and find forgiveness.

That, John Paul II was convinced, was why the face of the merciful Father had been turned toward the world *now*. The insight came from Poland; the need was universal.[4]

In Poland in the 1930s a young nun, Sister Faustina Kowalska—unsophisticated and with rudimentary education—had a series of visions in which Christ spoke to her of his great mercy. Outwardly cheerful and busy—her work at the convent involved cleaning and kitchen-work, serving food to the poor and answering the door to enquirers—Sister Faustina had a deep spiritual life and, after telling her confessor of some mystical experiences, she was ordered to keep a diary describing these.

On 2 February 1931, she described a vision:

> I saw the Lord Jesus clothed in a white garment. One hand was touching the garment at the breast. From beneath the garment ... there were emanating two large rays, one red the other pale ... After a while Jesus said to me 'Paint an image

according to the pattern you see, with the signature: Jesus I trust in you.'[5]

She also said that Christ had asked that the first Sunday after Easter be established as the Feast of Divine Mercy. The convent where Sister Faustina lived and worked was on the outskirts of Krakow. When she died on 5 October 1938, she was unknown except within her own community. Later, devotion to the Divine Mercy would spread rapidly across Poland, but first came the war years. During those years, the young Karol Wojtyła walked along this road on his way to work. Much later, he would recall:

> During the Nazi occupation, when I was working in the Solvay factory near here, I used to come here. Even now I recall the street that goes from Borek Falecki to Dębniki that I took every day going to work on the different turns with the wooden shoes on my feet. They're the shoes that we used to wear then. How was it possible to imagine that one day the man with the wooden shoes would consecrate the Basilica of the Divine Mercy at Lagiewniki of Krakow ...[6]

After the war, as information about Sister Faustina's visions spread, Karol Wojtyła as seminarian, priest and later as Bishop naturally came to hear of them and to take a great interest in the subject. Only someone with a lot to forgive can understand the sacrifice of personal animosity and resentment required to show mercy. When Karol Wojtyła came across the Divine Mercy devotion he was in the seminary, having lost all the people he loved, many by violence, and seen his beloved homeland occupied and terrorised by invaders. The need to forgive would seem especially poignant for Poles and it was particularly significant that it was to a Pole that this devotion was entrusted.

In the light of this, it is significant that Bishop Wojtyła was instrumental in composing the 1965 letter of forgiveness from the Polish bishops to the German bishops for atrocities committed in Poland 'we forgive and we ask for forgiveness ...' By contrast the atheistic authorities issued a counter blast: 'We do not forgive and we do not forget.' One cannot entirely blame anyone for feeling bitter with the memory of such brutality—John Paul II was later to call it 'bestiality'— but a desire for revenge, even if fulfilled, seldom brings the satisfaction hoped for: hence the need for reconciliation between nations as well as individuals. Forgiveness is an antidote to pride and a way of admitting that we are all sinners. The one who forgives does not condone the wrong done, but obeys the commandment of God and leaves it to God to be the judge.

If forgiveness can be hard, compassion also presents its own difficulties. It is easy to make soothing noises, but compassion means nothing unless it is accompanied by action, as shown by the parable of the Good Samaritan. It requires an openness to the suffering of others and not mere curiosity, as John Paul says, quoting *Gaudium et Spes*, man cannot 'find himself except through a sincere gift of himself'.[7]

Interest in the Divine Mercy spread rapidly across Poland in the post-war years, and copies of the picture, showing Christ with red and white rays flowing from his breast, became very popular. It all struck a deep chord—a longing for a sense of reassurance in Christ, the echoes of traditional devotion to the Sacred Heart, the tenderness of the message of mercy in a raw and wounded country where so many people were suffering and where there seemed so much cruelty, cynicism and evil. Along with the message about mercy came a chaplet of prayers, said on Rosary beads: on the Our Father bead: 'Eternal Father, I offer you the Body, Blood, Soul and Divinity of Your dearly beloved Son, in atonement for our sins and those of the whole world', and on the Hail Mary beads: 'For the sake of his sorrowful passion, have mercy on us and on the whole world', with a concluding prayer said three times: 'Holy God, Holy Mighty One, Holy Immortal One, have mercy on us and on the whole world.'

But the revelations did not find favour in Rome. It seems that the problem lay in a faulty translation of Sister Faustina's writings, and certainly this and other problems would have been made worse by the difficulty—at times amount to an impossibility—of proper communication with Poland in the 1950s and early 60s. The post was uncertain, telephones were often faulty or non-functioning and were also often tapped by the Communist authorities. The message of Divine Mercy was not complicated, but it seemed very much associated with a private revelation the details of which were hard to discover. Perhaps, too, the red-and-white colours of the Divine Mercy image evoked too easy a link with the national colours of Poland so that the devotion seemed linked with a longing for Polish freedom at a time of oppression. For whatever reasons, the message from Rome was clear: this was not an approved devotion and did not have the backing of formal Church authority.

But in the middle 1960s, Krakow had a new Archbishop who on his visits to Rome to sessions of the Vatican Council was able to set in motion the necessary detailed enquiries about Sister Faustina and the Divine

Mercy. Slowly, issues were clarified, accurate translations produced, and analyses made. By the early 1970s
the path had been cleared for this devotion to be given
formal approval. And in 1978, when John Paul was
elected Pope, he was able to take further decisive
action. As he would express it 'when I was called to
the See of Peter, I felt impelled to hand on those
experiences of a fellow Pole that deserve a place in the
treasury of the universal Church'.[8] In *Dives in Misericordia*, (1980) John Paul says that 'mercy is ... love's
second name.'[9]

Bishop Brendan Leahy notes that the emphasis on
mercy is part of a need to answer the needs of modern
man, who is puzzled about himself and needs a direct
personal relationship with God. Rules and regulations
and exhortations to good behaviour will not answer
this need: men feel themselves to be remote from God,
and there is an urgent need for them to rediscover God
even just to restore a sense of their own humanity:

> In presenting an encyclical on divine mercy,
> Pope John Paul is engaging with what he
> considers central to the Second Vatican Council:
> re-proposing the true face of God to today's
> humanity. As he puts it 'the more the Church's
> mission is centred upon humankind the more
> it must be confirmed and actualised theocentri-
> cally, that is to say, be directed in Jesus Christ
> to the Father. The [Second Vatican] Council saw
> the need for a new discovery of God. It saw as
> its task the proclamation of the Gospel that
> shows God is not a threat to human freedom
> but its fulfilment, because God is Love and
> Mercy. Divine love sets us free.'[10]

The message of Divine Mercy is the message of God's love. John Paul was very conscious that he was the Pope who was leading the Church across the threshold of a new Millennium. In the years to come, there would certainly be, he noted, 'no lack of difficult experiences'. A deep and trusting response to God's love would be more badly needed than ever. When canonising Sister Faustina and pondering the message of mercy, he could already see the threats to human life and human dignity that could dominate the twenty-first century. The call to respond to God's love was urgent:

> It is this love which must inspire humanity today, if it is to face the crisis of the meaning of life, the challenges of the most diverse needs and, especially, the duty to defend the dignity of every human person. Thus the message of divine mercy is also implicitly *a message about the value of every human being.* Each person is precious in God's eyes; Christ gave his life for each one; to everyone the Father gives his Spirit and offers intimacy.[11]

The message is a challenging one, but the need to respond is great: a world community which lacks an understanding of love and mercy will be a place of horror, but one which is open to God and able to responds to him can face the future with hope:

> It is not easy to love with a deep love, which lies in the authentic gift of self. This love can only be learned by penetrating the mystery of God's love. Looking at him, being one with his fatherly heart, we are able to look with new eyes at our brothers and sisters, with an attitude of unselfishness and solidarity, of generosity and forgiveness. All this is mercy![12]

John Paul made all this his own: he lived it in his life with his forgiveness of the man who tried to kill him, and he taught it with conviction, seeing himself as a sinner in need of mercy, and the world as being in need of mercy.

> We must personally experience this mercy if in turn we want to be capable of mercy. Let us learn to forgive! The spiral of hatred and violence which stains with blood the path of so many individuals and nations can only be broken by the miracle of forgiveness.[13]

Pope John Paul II is sometimes described as the 'Mercy Pope'. He promoted and lived the message throughout his priesthood, and he instituted the Feast of Mercy on the second Sunday of Easter, as requested by Christ in the visions to Sister Faustina. He was to die on the vigil of the Feast on 2 April 2005.

St Faustina's Diary has an entry which has provoked a good deal of discussion. In 1938 she noted that Christ had told her he had a special love for Poland: 'From her will come forth the spark that will prepare the world for my final coming.'[14] Was this 'spark' the devotion to the Divine Mercy, made known to the world by a Polish Pope?

Notes

[1]   John Paul II, *Redemptor Hominis*, (1979), 1.
[2]   John Paul II, *Dives in Misericordia*, (1980), 2.
[3]   John Paul II, *Homily at the Mass of canonisation of St Faustina*, (30 April 2000).
[4]   G. Weigel, *First Things* (27 April 2011).
[5]   Sister Faustina, *Diary: Divine Mercy in my soul* (Stockbridge: Marian Press, 2011), p. 24.
[6]   John Paul II, *Homily at the canonisation of St Faustina* (30 April 2000).

7   John Paul II, *Dives in Misericordia* (1980), 24.

8   John Paul II, *Memory and Identity* (New York: Rizzoli, 2005), p. 6.

9   John Paul II, *Dives in Misericordia*, 7

10   B. Leahy, *Believe in Love: The Life, Ministry and Teachings of John Paul II* (Dublin: Veritas, 2011), p. 34.

11   John Paul II, *Homily at the canonisation of St Faustina* (30 April 2000).

12   *Ibid.*

13   John Paul II, *Regina Coeli Address* (23 April 1995).

14   Sister Faustina, *Diary*, 1732, p. 612.

10

MEN AND WOMEN, AND THE THEOLOGY OF THE BODY

WHY ARE WE male and female? Are there any essential differences between the two sexes or are we actually identical and interchangeable, except for a few trifling differences of internal plumbing?

These questions were being asked in the West in the early 1980s, when the sexual revolution plus feminism combined to foster the idea that a unisex culture—one with all differences between males and females minimised if not actually abolished in law and language and social customs—would create a form of utopia. And the idea has lingered. Earlier campaigners for women's rights in the first half of the twentieth century had sought opportunities for university education and called for a fair deal for women who were being paid much less than men for identical work, and urged changes in the law so that women could enter professions such as banking and teaching on equal terms. But by the 1980s a rigid feminist ideology had taken over, and achieved much success within the bureaucracies of many Western nations. Schools were being urged to teach distorted versions of history in order that a feminist line was announced (Britain's Equal Opportunities Commission produced a series of orders instructing schools to teach female American Indian Chiefs and female pirates) and distorted versions of human biology in order to obey the official line (the

Equal Opportunities Commission again, urging that pictures and wall friezes showing 'parenting activities' should show men and women doing all tasks, including feeding babies ...).

When John Paul gave his lengthy series of teachings on what came to be called 'The theology of the body', it was assumed by commentators that this was just the Pope re-affirming the traditional Christian moral message on sexual morality. And the commentators were in fact few—for some journalists and broadcasters, the teaching given in some 130 Wednesday audiences spread over a period of years went largely unnoticed.[1] But for others, including large numbers of younger Catholics in the New Movements in the Church, the message opened up wide horizons and a vision of a topic of huge importance. The Theology of the Body is no mere re-statement of Christian sexual morality but a profound examination of what it means to be male and female.

Why was Christ male? Why was it important for God to become incarnate as a human man, and not as a woman? What was Christ teaching us when he spoke about himself as the Bridegroom and the Church as his Bride? Where does Mary fit into all of this? Why is marriage so important, and why is our relationship with God so often taught as being that of children to a beloved father? Why is marriage a sacrament? Can it sanctify the world, and if so, how?

For John Paul, an authentic understanding of the nature of the human person was central to good theology. A study of human beings, male and female, revealed the mystery: created in the image of God, having a dignity of infinite worth, too often subjected to degradation and misery in the twentieth century, human beings are beloved by God and have the capacity not only to love him in return but to communicate this love to one another and to build up a civilisation based on love.

Being a male or a female, John Paul taught, is not some sort of optional extra to personhood, but is of the essence. Maleness and femaleness is 'in some way is "constitutive of the person" (not only "an attribute of the person")'.[2] He had emphasised this when writing *Love and Responsibility* many years earlier: the book explores questions about love, sex, relationships and marriage in depth. Being a man, or being a woman, is part of our identity,[3] and accepting our identity is central to our relationship with one another and with God.

The discussions in the Catholic Church about sexual morality during the twentieth century had tended to focus on the idea of 'rules'. The Church, many people believed, had a set of rules and regulations relating to sex and marriage: these rules were not necessarily arbitrary, and they related to God's best plans for us as revealed in the Scriptures and the consistent teaching of the Church. But they were nonetheless essentially rules and the point therefore was either to show the importance of obeying them or find some way around them, or—possibly—to set about lobbying in order to get them changed. It was in this climate that Pope Paul VI's great encyclical *Humanae Vitae* was published, and when it reaffirmed the teaching that artificial contraception is always and everywhere wrong, the reaction among many clergy and committed laity—articulated with great passion on television and radio and in colleges and seminaries and in books and academic work across the Western world—was one of dismay that the Pope had failed to 'update the rules'. It was clear that in the minds of many, this issue was connected with regulations such as those governing, for example, the Eucharistic fast (reduced during the twentieth century from fasting from midnight to fasting for one hour before receiving Holy Communion) or Friday penance.

Karol Wojtyła had been among those deeply connected with the work and study that preceded the publication of *Humanae Vitae*. His concern for helping married couples was forged in the pastoral challenges presented by the very difficult conditions of post-war Poland, where under a Communist regime housing was poor and wartime damage slow to be repaired, with families living in overcrowded flats and working in rough and dangerous conditions for poor wages that bought only limited amounts of rationed food and household necessities. To emphasise the beauty of family life under such conditions—especially where the teaching had for long years previously been poor as common values had been assumed and a Christian way of life transmitted seamlessly from one generation to the next—was crucial and demanded a new approach. Karol Wojtyła rooted his work as a pastor in a profound respect for parenthood and for family life, and in the practical experience of years as a Catholic layman in wartime who knew about hunger, cold, work, friendship, poor living conditions, and the value of life and love. He had great faith in the power of the witness of married people in showing the richness of Christianity. He taught that profound issues relating to human identity and human worth were at stake when contraception was introduced, and he called for authentic and challenging teaching to enable families to be open to life and to recognise the dangers to marital unity and fidelity inherent in the contraceptive mentality.

As Pope his Theology of the Body built on all of this. Our bodies, our identity as male and female, have a built-in message about who we are and how we can love and help one another. Love is by its nature faithful and fruitful. Contraception offends against the unity of the marriage bond and against the dignity of the human person.

John Paul's deep respect for women and his ease of friendship with them was a part of all of this. Unlike many clergy of his generation and of those immediately preceding it, he had not been formed and trained in a seminary from a young age—instead he had spent some formative years as a Catholic layman, working in a drama group with young men and women, forging deep and lasting friendships there, sharing in the everyday life of a generation struggling together in wartime. As a priest and as a Bishop, he was active teaching young people and leading youth groups— whether it was as a teacher at the Catholic University at Lublin, or leading young people on hikes and canoeing trips in the countryside, or pastoral work in Krakow, he was at ease with both women and men.

John Paul's Marian theology met his understanding of the need to engage with the feminist movement and with the whole question of male/female relationships and their spiritual message. A major encyclical *Mulieris Dignitatem*, issued in 1988, broke new ground in exploring these issues. For John Paul, the key to understanding the subject lies in looking at the mystery of the human person, and looking at it from 'the beginning', the opening words of both the Book of Genesis and the Gospel of John:

> Let us enter into the setting of the biblical
> 'beginning' ...; the human race, which takes its
> origin from the calling into existence of man
> and woman, crowns the whole work of crea-
> tion; both man and woman are human beings
> to an equal degree, both are created in God's
> image.[4]

Looking at the images of God in the Old Testament, at
Jesus' relationships with women in the New, at the
damage caused by sin, at the spiritual significance of
virginity and of motherhood, and at the huge significance of Mary, John Paul creates a richly textured
discussion about women. It is soaked in Biblical
references and with an analysis of the importance of
motherhood and fatherhood, of marriage and of
pregnancy, with a frankness and depth that is not
found in nineteenth century or early twentieth century
Papal writings on these subjects. There is an absence
of easy assumptions and of sentimental statements,
and a strong affirmation of the beauty of motherhood—including spiritual motherhood—and the
dignity that it confers on women. He was writing just
as various techniques of artificial reproduction—'test
tube babies' and so on—were beginning to be not only
possible but popularised, and *Mulieris Dignitatem* is at
once a profound statement of what it means to be fully
human, and a plea that this full humanity be respected
and understood. It was a plea that was to fall on too
many ears in the West that were deaf. But in developing countries, where the Church will be shaping the
destiny of nations and cultures for years to come, there
was interest and even fascination among Catholic
women who were beginning to emerge as doctors,

educators, academics, counsellors, and holders of public office at local and national levels.

In 1995 John Paul issued a *Letter to Women* which began with a rather moving 'thank you' to women in different walks of life, noting the rich contribution that women make and have made to societies down the centuries.

> I know of course that simply saying thank you is not enough. Unfortunately, we are heirs to a history which has *conditioned* us to a remarkable extent. In every time and place, this condition-ing has been an obstacle to the progress of women. Women's dignity has often been unac-knowledged and their prerogatives misrepre-sented; they have often been relegated to the margins of society and even reduced to servi-tude. This has prevented women from truly being themselves and it has resulted in a spirit-ual impoverishment of humanity. Certainly it is no easy task to assign the blame for this, considering the many kinds of cultural condi-tioning which down the centuries have shaped ways of thinking and acting. And if objective blame, especially in particular historical con-texts, has belonged to not just a few members of the Church, for this I am truly sorry. May this regret be transformed, on the part of the whole Church, into a renewed commitment of fidelity to the Gospel vision. When it comes to setting women free from every kind of exploitation and domination, the Gospel contains an ever rele-vant message which goes back to the *attitude of Jesus Christ himself.* Transcending the estab-lished norms of his own culture, Jesus treated women with openness, respect, acceptance and tenderness. In this way he honoured the dignity

which women have always possessed according to God's plan and in his love.[5]

After facing the reality of history with courage, John Paul spoke about the Church's real contribution to the dignity of women, and gave a strong message to the world:

> As far as personal rights are concerned, there is an urgent need to achieve *real equality* in every area: equal pay for equal work, protection for working mothers, fairness in career advancements, equality of spouses with regard to family rights and the recognition of everything that is part of the rights and duties of citizens in a democratic State.[6]

John Paul spoke of the 'genius of women' or the 'feminine genius', in a phrase that began to be used by Catholic writers and academics and looks set to inspire women, both Catholic and non-Catholic, exploring the topics of gender and sexual difference in the twenty-first century and beyond.

> Necessary emphasis should be placed on the *genius of women*, not only by considering great and famous women of the past or present, but also those *ordinary* women who reveal the gift of their womanhood by placing themselves at the service of others in their everyday lives ... Perhaps more than men, women *acknowledge the person,* because they see persons with their hearts. They see them independently of various ideological or political systems. They see others in their greatness and limitations; they try to go out to them and *help them.* In this way the basic plan of the Creator takes flesh in the history of humanity and there is constantly revealed, in

> the variety of vocations, that *beauty*-not merely
> physical, but above all spiritual-which God
> bestowed from the very beginning on all, and
> in a particular way on women.[7]

John Paul's letter was a specific contribution to the
United Nations Conference on Women being held in
China in 1995. The anomaly of holding the conference
in a country famous for forcing women through
dangerous, painful, and humiliating abortions that
threatened their lives and wrecked their health, was
lost on well-to-do Western commentators who
assumed that imposing a 'one child policy' was something that the Chinese rulers should be allowed to
impose on hapless young women.

But, thanks to the vigorous approach taken by John
Paul and a gifted, intelligent and courageous team, the
conference took an unexpected turn. A delegation from
the Vatican, led by American legal scholar Mary Ann
Glendon, went to this conference, and succeeded in
drawing attention to the absurdity of the attempts by
various Western nations to impose contraception and
abortion on impoverished nations which desperately
sought women's access to basic necessities such as
clean water, food, simple health care, education, and
adequate housing.

The problem of forced abortions and sterilisations
was not resolved, but the coercive campaigners at the
United Nations, backed by massive funds and the
ruthless political machinations of Western nations, did
not see the conference go fully their way. Over the next
years, things in China would in any case change
radically, and as the second decade of the twenty-first
century opened, and the tragedy of the country's
ageing population began to be fully recognised, poli-

cies started to change. History will not treat the abortionists of China well, and the massive numbers of Catholics in China, rising year on year, show who will be writing the history and creating the culture of China in the years ahead.

But the tragedy for men and women in the West, struggling to find a way forward in the sexual chaos of the early twenty-first century, is that the rich, interesting and important debate about what it means to be male and female, initiated by John Paul II in his 'Theology of the Body' was sidelined because commentators were obsessed with their own enthusiasm for contraception and could not look seriously at other subjects related to male/female issues.

The topic of the nature of the Church herself, of her priests, of the maleness of Christ and of the Apostles (in a part of the world where all pagan religions had priestesses and it would have been normal for the early Christians to have created women priests) was reduced by too many media commentators to a rushed set of clichés of mind-numbing tedium. A sort of repetitive mantra that went 'John Paul is anti-woman—he refuses to listen to women—he is an old-fashioned Pole who thinks women are inferior—he knows no theology' would be trotted out on radio and TV debates along with assertions that "of course" all this would change with the next Pope ...

Meanwhile, the West—a dying Europe with families in crisis, fewer and fewer children being born and a massive cultural shift as countries acquired massive Islamic populations in their cities to sustain economic growth—desperately needed a new understanding of the whole male/female mystery and simply tried to block it all out in a barrage of consumerism, greed, advertising, TV soap operas, and health fads.

The *Catechism of the Catholic Church* teaches that: 'As being at once body and spirit, man expresses and perceives spiritual realities through physical signs and symbols'[8]. John Paul teaches this with depth and vigour:

> The body, in fact, and only the body, is capable of making visible what is invisible: the spiritual and the divine. It has been created to transfer into the visible reality of the world the mystery hidden from eternity in God and thus to be a sign of it.[9]

Male and female, marriage, the dignity of the human body and the truths it conveys about our human reality: these are truths that we need to rediscover. Christopher West, one of the foremost writers on this topic who along with others has been inspired by John Paul's Theology of the Body and believes it holds the key to sanity in a confused culture:

> We who have been raised with 'materialism' on the one hand and 'spiritualism' on the other must say it again and again until it sinks in and transforms us … the marriage of the flesh and the spirit lies at the heart of the Gospel and at the heart of our humanity.[10]

John Paul describes marriage as the 'primordial sacrament', in words which echo back to St Paul and his emphasis on marriage as the 'great mystery' linked deeply with Christ and the Church. Bridegroom and Bride, Man and Woman, Christ and the Church: marriage is 'the fundamental, first and original revelation of the divine Mystery inscribed in the very order of creation' (West)[11]. The mystery of redemption in Christ 'clothes itself' says John Paul 'in the figure and form of the primordial sacrament'.[12]

Male and female are not artificial constructs. Our bodies hold a mystery which we must explore with reverence. John Paul looked at this subject as no Pope had ever done before. From 'the beginning' —John Paul always emphasised the human person as being there in the Divine plan from the start—God wanted us to understand this. Now, at a time when our failure to do so imperils our very future, with attempts to redefine humanity itself to conform to strict ideological rules, we need to study and apply John Paul's message on all of this.

Emily Stimpson writes

> the differences between men and women aren't meant to divide us; they're intended to unite us. They're complementary. The way we love, reason and create, the way we live in the world as women or men, is enriched by the way the other sex does the same. It's made complete, whole and perfect in company with the other.[13]

The mystery of male and female, the embodied greatness of the human person, and the joyful living out of this reality in the gift of people in service and love at so many levels, is a vision of humanity that a bleak Western modern world, obsessed with a mixture of trivia and real fear for the human future in a greedy world, needs with a great ache. John Paul, exploring the meaning of who we are, and our dignity 'from the beginning', has given us a key to a sane future.

Notes

1 The addresses were given over a period of years in Papal audiences from 1979 to 1984. See G. Weigel, *Witness to Hope: The Biography of Pope John Paul II*, pp. 335-336.

2 Pope John Paul II, *Theology of the Body*, 10:1

3 Wojtyła notes that "This fact is not contradicted [those rare cases of] hermaphrodism—any more than any other sickness or deformity militates against the fact that there is such a thing as human nature" (*Love and Responsibility* (London: Collins, 1981), p. 47.

4 John Paul II, *Mulieris Dignitatem*, 6.

5 John Paul II, *Letter to Women* (3 June 1995).

6 *Ibid.*, 4.

7 *Ibid.*, 12.

8 *Catechism of the Catholic Church*, 1146.

9 John Paul II, *Theology of the Body*, 19:4.

10 C. West, *At the Heart of the Gospel: Reclaiming the Body for the New Evangelisation* (New York: Image Books 2012), p. 59.

11 *Ibid.*, p. 111.

12 *Ibid.*

13 E. Stimpson, *These Beautiful Bones, An Everyday Theology of the Body* (Steubenville: Emmaus Road Publishing), p. 30.

11

Finding Meaning in Suffering

At present I rejoice when I suffer for you; I complete in my own flesh what is lacking in the sufferings of Christ for the sake of his body, which is the Church.

Colossians 1:24

 HESE MYSTERIOUS WORDS from St Paul are the clearest Scriptural description of what is known as Redemptive Suffering; that is, 'offering up' for the good of others anything from mild annoyances to terminal illness. The Bible deals extensively with suffering; the Book of Job, for example, takes this as its theme, but only in the New Testament is the notion of participation in the suffering of the Messiah for the good of others. For whenever the sufferings of Christ overflow to us, so, through Christ, a great comfort also overflows. So if we are afflicted, it is for your comfort and salvation, and if we receive comfort it is also for you. You may experience the same comfort when you come to endure the same sufferings we endure. Our hope for you is most firm, just as you share in our sufferings, so shall you also share in our consolation' (2 Co 1:5-7).

In his life, Karol Wojtyła saw loss in all its contexts: of family, nation, health. Yet he never lost heart though he must at times have wondered 'why'? It was no coincidence that his Apostolic Letter *Salvifici Doloris* (On the Christian Meaning of Human Suffering) was issued in 1984, designated as the Year of the Redemption.

> Every man has his own share in the Redemption
> ... He is called to share in that suffering through
> which all human suffering has also been
> redeemed. In bringing about the Redemption
> through suffering, Christ has also raised human
> suffering to the level of the Redemption. Thus
> each man, in his suffering, can also become a
> sharer in the redemptive suffering of Christ.[1]

The Holy Father turns to the problem of evil, which
brings with it sin and death and is only conquered by
the Cross. Loss of eternal life is the definitive suffering,
but Christ's salvific Passion strikes evil at its root. We
can even say that Christ's offering us a chance to share
in his suffering gives us also a chance to combat and
overcome evil in the world.

All who suffer in secret will receive a special grace
'of interior maturity and spiritual greatness'.[2] It takes
time to make sense of one's own suffering, which can
only be resolved by looking to the Crucified who does
not answer directly, but gradually makes clear what
the Holy Father calls a vocation:

> For it is above all a call. It is a vocation. Christ
> does not explain in the abstract the reasons for
> suffering, but before all else he says 'Follow me!
> Come! Take part through your suffering in this
> work of saving the world, a salvation achieved
> through my suffering! Through my Cross.'

Suffering as a vocation is certainly not new, many of
the great saints have been 'victim souls', such as
Therese of Lisieux, Gemma Galgani, Faustina Kowalska and Padre Pio. Suffering has also been a charism

of Mother Teresa's Missionaries of Charity. An early would-be sister was saddened that her health prevented her from joining the order. Mother Teresa asked her to return home and offer up her sufferings instead and from that time onward, each sister was expected to have one sick or suffering co-worker. After her death it was revealed that for fifty years Mother Teresa carried an interior cross, the desolate loneliness of spiritual aridity, a suffering which bore great fruit for her order.

Karol Wojtyła came to believe important events in his life were connected with the death or suffering of individuals close to him. His own father's death and the illness and death of Jan Tyranowski accompanied his vocation to the priesthood—the only relative present at his ordination was his godmother. In 1967 Archbishop Wojtyła was named cardinal and left for Rome; his friend Father Marian Jaworski took his place on a pastoral visitation but on the journey he was involved in a train accident and lost his hand.

Pope John Paul II's first act as Pope was to visit his friend Bishop Andrzej Maria Deskur who was in the Gemelli hospital in Rome, having suffered a stroke. When he arrived home, Bishop Deskur found a letter from the Holy Father; 'Now you know what your mission in the Church is ...' This mission of prayer for the Pope and his ministry would continue until the death of John Paul and into the pontificate of Benedict XVI. Deskur was thus the Pope's 'suffering co-worker'. A letter recently made public from the Holy Father, sent to Deskur on his birthday in 2004, includes the words

> Thank you, first of all, for the support you have
> given me in my service at the Apostolic See with

> the suffering you have borne in your silent com-
> mitment to Christ and His Mother, in your con-
> stant prayer and spirit of love for the Church ...[3]

Both Jaworski and Deskur would be made Cardinals by the Holy Father.

If the Pope felt accompanied in his ministry by the loss and suffering of others, he would in turn offer himself as a living sacrifice. To understand more deeply his identification with suffering, it is necessary to look at the belief many Poles had of the unique role of suffering of the Polish people.

One of Poland's greatest writers, Adam Mickiewicz, writing in the early nineteenth century, developed the idea of Poland, the Christ of Nations. By this he meant that Poland's long history of suffering could be made sense of and interpreted in the light of the Cross. Suffering was, he believed, Poland's mission for the salvation of her people and the world. If Poland had a messianic role, it was not to replace Christ nor the Jewish people; Mickiewicz believed that Israel (which did not then exist on the map) as well as Poland had a leading role in the future. The metaphor was not accepted by everyone, but the idea has sustained many Poles throughout their most difficult years. Partition (removal of Christ's garments), betrayal or silence of friends, exile, mockery and torture by occupiers—if all this was Golgotha then Resurrection would come eventually, 'just as bloody sacrifices on earth ended with the Resurrection of Christ, so wars in Christianity will cease with the resurrection of the Polish nation'.[4]

As we have seen (Chapter 6) this sense of national destiny was shared by others. But the poet Juliusz Slowacki, had a rather different prophecy. A poem well-known to Wojtyła, *The Slavic Pope*, published in

1848, celebrates a future Slav Pope who, by his courage, leadership and charisma would sweep away tyrants, bring healing, freedom and joy to all and renew the life of the Church. How much was Slowacki able to see into the future? Or could it have been wishful thinking, a happy thought in the face of so much bad news? The Europe of the late eighteenth to early nineteenth century saw plenty of this kind of mysticism, much of it secular, but in Poland the religious imagination was always stronger.

Professor Eamon Duffy, the historian, recalls that after a talk he had given in 1978, just after the election of Pope John Paul II, an elderly Polish academic in exile, came up to him:

> And I rapidly became convinced that this man was mad. I said to him, 'You must be very pleased to have had a Polish pope elected'. And he said, 'More than pleased, the world is about to be changed ... It is prophesied that when there is a Polish pope, Russian tyranny will fall, Communism will fall, and there will be a great re-evangelisation of the Slav peoples, which will be led by Poland. And that is a prelude to the end of the world.' And I backed away from this man, I hastily changed the subject. And, in 1989, I remembered all that ...[5]

A sense of destiny would accompany Karol Wojtyła throughout his papacy. On his election, Cardinal Wyszynski had told him that he would be the Pope who would lead the Church into the next millennium. He would later say

> I understand that I have to lead Christ's church into the third millennium by prayer, by various programs. But I saw that this is not going to be

enough. She must be led by suffering. By sacrifice. The Pope has to be attacked. The Pope has
to suffer. So that every family may see that there
is a higher gospel, the gospel of suffering, by
which the future is prepared.[6]

No Polish pope then would expect to assume the
papacy without suffering. We would all shortly find
out what this meant.

On 13 May 1981, as the Popemobile drove slowly
through the adoring crowds in St Peter's Square, two
gunshots rang out, and amid the horrified screams of
onlookers, the Holy Father slumped into the arms of
his secretary Mgr Dziwisz. The Pope said later that
through his fading consciousness he had a sense that
his life would be spared. The following day it was
announced that Cardinal Wyszyński was dying from
stomach and lymphatic cancer—again a great loss at
a momentous time in the Holy Father's life. As he was
recovering in hospital, Pope John Paul spoke to his old
friend by telephone, bed to bed, and on 28 May the
Cardinal died.

Four months later, at his first public appearance in
St Peter's Square, John Paul told pilgrims:

> During the last months God permitted me to
> experience suffering and the danger of losing my
> life. He also allowed me to understand clearly
> ... that this was one of his special graces for me
> as a man and at the same time ... for the Church.

More ill-health followed, there were complications
following the surgery to remove the bullet. The Pope
had had contracted an infection that required more
surgery, possibly transmitted via a blood transfusion.
In fact, although not immediately obvious, the near-

fatal shooting compromised his health and he was never again to enjoy the robustness that he had enjoyed during the first sixty-one years of his life. But the Pope was not one to let bouts of illness hold him back and for more than twenty years he pushed himself to the limits of his physical strength.

However from the 1990s his health began to decline; he suffered from an intestinal tumour, several falls (one resulting in a broken femur) and an appendectomy. By the end of the decade he had a marked tremor which was confirmed as Parkinson's Disease in 2001. He was probably in constant pain with arthritis. Although the Parkinson's slowly deprived him of movement and speech, the Holy Father continued to be seen in public. It was, as Archbishop Angelo Comastri said, that with his suffering John Paul II wrote the most beautiful encyclical of his life. A less courageous person would have hidden from public view but the Holy Father had still much to teach us.

In his very public suffering the Pope was teaching the world a valuable lesson in the preciousness of all life. Having spoken against 'the Culture of Death' for so long, he showed that even when reduced to a wheelchair and barely able to speak, a life still had meaning and even dignity. No human life is ever worthless, however incapacitated by pain and suffering, however inconvenient to others. If, during the early years of his Pontificate, Karol Wojtyła had showed us how to live, now in the extreme infirmity of old age he was showing us how to die. It was a lesson that the world, obsessed with image, youth and glamour, needed to hear. In his life and in his death, we saw the true value of a life lived for and with God.

Suffering is never easy and it would be wrong to assume that because the Holy Father had reached an intimacy with God shared by very few, he did not resent the limitations imposed by bad health. After a trachaeotomy at the beginning of 2005 rendering him unable to speak, he wrote on a piece of paper, 'What have they done to me? Still, I am always *totus tuus*.'

By Good Friday of 2005, the Pope was unable to attend the Way of the Cross in person, so he participated via a television link from the Apostolic Palace. Towards the end of the meditations someone placed a large crucifix on the Holy Father's lap and at the station where Jesus dies on the Cross he embraced it tightly, wordlessly clinging to it, his whole being united to the suffering Christ recalling St Paul's words 'I have been crucified with *Christ*. It is no longer I who live, but *Christ* who *lives in me*' (Ga 2:20). Through the course of his whole life, Karol Wojtyła was dedicated to living in and for Christ; by the end, he had become a living icon of the Suffering Lord.

Even in his silence, the Pope was still able to teach us. Cardinal Ratzinger described this very well in his sermon preached at the funeral of John Paul II: 'in this very communion with the suffering Lord, tirelessly and with renewed intensity, he proclaimed the Gospel, the mystery of that love which goes to the end'.[7]

As John Paul's favourite spiritual master John of the Cross said 'in the end we will be examined in love'. It was love which drove him on even when his legs could no longer bear him; love for God, the church and all the people of the world. And at the end the world seemed to understand and respond as the cries of 'Santo subito!' rang out around St Peter's Square.

Notes

1   Pope John Paul II, *Salvifici Doloris*, 19.
2   *Ibid.*, 28.
3   W. Redzioch, *L'Osservatore Romano*, 10 September 2011.
4   See A. Mickiewicz, *Pan Tadeusz* (Paris, 1834).
5   E. Duffy, *Interview on Pope John Paul II: The Millennial Pope* as found on http://www.pbs.org/wgbh/pages/frontline/shows /pope /interviews/duffy.html.
6   *Ibid.*
7   Cardinal Joseph Ratzinger, *Homily at Funeral of Pope John Paul II*, 8 April 2005.

12

THE EUCHARIST

OHN PAUL II celebrated Mass in more places across the globe than any priest in history. As he travelled the world on pilgrimage, he used altars set up in places that included sports arenas, airfields, exhibition centres and racecourses as well as churches and chapels and cathedrals. As a seminarian, he had attended Mass in the Archbishop's Palace with its own beautiful chapel—but in secrecy and in danger, in an occupied country in wartime. As a young priest, he celebrated Mass in a country church, in a busy city church crowded with students, and with young people on hiking and canoeing trips with an altar formed of an upturned canoe and a Cross made of paddles lashed together.

And always, the Mass was the centre of his life. For John Paul, the Mass was not simply something that a priest 'did': it was not a tradition or an obligation or a ritual, or a mere symbol associated with something spiritual. It was at the very core of what it meant to be a Christian, and in that sense the very core of the bond between God and man. 'This varied scenario of celebrations of the Eucharist has given me a powerful experience of its universal and, so to speak, cosmic character. Yes, cosmic! Because even when it is celebrated on the humble altar of a country church, the Eucharist is always in some way celebrated *on the altar of the world*. It unites heaven and earth. It embraces and permeates all creation.'[1]

That encyclical letter just quoted, *Ecclesia de Eucharistia* (2003) was his last, written towards the end of his long life. In it, he emphasised: 'The Church draws her life from the Eucharist, and he spoke of a memorable experience:

> During the Great Jubilee of the Year 2000 I had an opportunity to celebrate the Eucharist in the Cenacle of Jerusalem where, according to tradition, it was first celebrated by Jesus himself. *The Upper Room was where this most holy Sacrament was instituted...* I am grateful to the Lord Jesus for allowing me to repeat in that same place, in obedience to his command: 'Do this in memory of me' (Lk 22:19), the words which he spoke two thousand years ago.[2]

When John Paul was elected to the Papacy in 1978, it was at a time when many in the Church seemed uncertain about the importance of the Eucharist, and about its centrality in the life of the Church and of every Christian. Although the Second Vatican Council had spoken of the Eucharist as 'the source and summit of the Christian life', there were voices that were suggesting that what mattered was simply the gathering of people together in a community for fellowship, with broken bread as a symbol of goodwill and solidarity, or who downplayed the presence of Christ or celebrated the Eucharist with disdain for liturgical norms and with trite and silly music.

When John Paul celebrated Mass he did so with a prayerful intensity which was noticed by all present. This was especially evident at his early morning Masses in Rome. Previous Popes had tended to regard morning Mass as essentially something private, perhaps not even shared with members of the house-

hold. John Paul's morning Masses were open to invited
guests. This did not make the occasion a very public
one: those invited were people who had some special
reason for the invitation—involvement with some
Catholic group or organisation, or attendance at some
special conference, etc. But, essentially, it did mean
that ordinary faithful Catholics from around the world
were, by invitation, able to attend Mass celebrated by
the Bishop of Rome, in the heart of Rome, at the start
of his working day. This sent a powerful message
about the centrality of the Mass, at a time when its
importance in the life of the Church was being sidelined by some commentators.

Those who attended such Masses often spoke
afterwards of the care and solemnity with which John
Paul approached the Eucharist: prayerful preparation,
a celebration of serene intensity, a long thanksgiving
afterwards.

At great public Masses, the numbers present could
exceed three or four million. For the vast majority, the
altar was seen only as something in a remote distance,
but drawn closer by means of large television screens.
John Paul was the first Pope in history to have the use
of such technology at his disposal: the large-scale
Mass, with the drama of the Host held high before
millions, and Holy Communion being distributed by
hundreds of priests, while surging crowds were mar-
shalled by stewards, became a feature of his pontificate.

Of course this brought its own problems. Not all the
Masses were dignified, not all that happened was
reverent. Sometimes the music chosen was simply
unsuitable, or aspects of the liturgy became absurd as
organisers sought to incorporate activities deemed to
be of local importance. Sometimes, efforts to include

the maximum number of different groups of singers, readers, etc seemed to overshadow the Mass itself. John Paul always seemed oblivious to all of this. Regardless of what vestments he had to wear — sometimes magnificent and beautiful, sometimes definitely not — or what music or gimmicks he had to endure, it was always evident that he was simply deeply immersed in the great reality of the Mass itself.

He was not, however, unaware of the problems of tasteless gimmicks attached to the Mass, or of the — more serious — abandonment of liturgical rules and norms in too many parishes and Catholic institutions during the 1980s.

From the beginning of his pontificate, he instituted an annual *Letter to Priests* on Holy Thursday. In 1980 this included a call for Eucharistic adoration — the exposing of the Blessed Sacrament in a monstrance on the altar for a prolonged period of prayer. This was a practice that had fallen into disuse, especially in Europe, at this time, and John Paul's revival of it became something of a hallmark of his pontificate.

'Public and private devotion to the Holy Eucharist outside Mass is highly recommended' he urged 'for the presence of Christ, who is adored by the faithful in the Sacrament, derives from the sacrifice and is directed towards sacramental and spiritual communion.'

> The Church and the world have great need of Eucharistic adoration. Jesus waits for us in this sacrament of love. Let us be generous with our time in going to meet Him in adoration and contemplation full of faith. And let us be ready to make reparation for the great faults and

crimes of the world. May our adoration never cease.[3]

He was repeating the message a decade and a half later, by which time many groups in the Church—especially among the young—had revived the practice of Eucharistic adoration and were making it their own. The New Movements, in particular, were making it a feature of their conferences, retreats, and rallies. But there was still some resistance—again notably in the 'old' countries of Europe, and it was in a letter specifically addressed to bishops in Belgium that he raised the subject again:

> Closeness to the Eucharistic Christ in silence and contemplation does not distance us from our contemporaries but, on the contrary, makes us open to human joy and distress, broadening our hearts on a global scale. Through adoration the Christian mysteriously contributes to the radical transformation of the world and to the sowing of the gospel. Anyone who prays to the Eucharistic Saviour draws the whole world with him and raises it to God.[4]

John Paul never saw adoration of Christ in the Eucharist as a private devotion that involved a retreat from the obligation to Christian service: on the contrary, it was from unity with Christ in the Eucharist that the Christian should draw strength and fresh zeal for missionary work, for love and service of neighbour, and for the courage needed to face daily life and the trials that inevitably come along:

> The authentic sense of the Eucharist becomes of itself the school of active love for neighbour. We know that this is the true and full order of

love that the Lord has taught us: 'By this love
you have for one another, everyone will know
that you are my disciples.' The Eucharist edu-
cates us to this love in a deeper way; it shows
us, in fact, what value each person, our brother
or sister, has in God's eyes, if Christ offers
Himself equally to each one, under the species
of bread and wine. If our Eucharistic worship
is authentic, it must make us grow in awareness
of the dignity of each person. The awareness of
that dignity becomes the deepest motive of our
relationship with our neighbour.[5]

To the end of his life, John Paul showed his devotion
to Christ in the Eucharist by his physical actions. When
physically frail, he still attempted to get on to his
knees—memorably when taking part in a Corpus
Christi procession where he was seated before a
prie-dieu and struggled to kneel, saying 'But Jesus is
here—please!' When at a Mass celebrated by Cardinal
Ratzinger, he made a great effort to kneel to receive
Holy Communion from him, even though it obviously
caused him difficulty and pain.

For John Paul, the Eucharist was a constant in his
life, binding his priesthood to cherished childhood
memories. In 1994, in a special *Letter to Children* written
during the International Year of the Family, he shared
memories of his own First Communion day:

Every boy and every girl belonging to a Catholic family knows all about this custom: First
Holy Communion is a great family celebration.
On that day, together with the one who is
making his or her First Holy Communion, the
parents, brothers, sisters, relatives, godparents,
and sometimes also the instructors and teachers, generally receive the Eucharist. The day of

First Holy Communion is also a great day of celebration in the parish. I remember as though it were yesterday when, together with the other boys and girls of my own age, I received the Eucharist for the first time in the parish church of my town. This event is usually commemorated in a family photo, so that it will not be forgotten. Photos like these generally remain with a person all through his or her life. As time goes by, people take out these pictures and experience once more the emotions of those moments; they return to the purity and joy experienced in that meeting with Jesus, the one who out of love became the Redeemer of Man.[6]

From Wadowice in Poland in the 1920s, to St Peter's in Rome in the twenty-first century, John Paul's life was bound up with the Eucharist. He received the Viaticum on the eve of Divine Mercy Sunday, 2005, as he lay dying: Mass was celebrated in his room by Archbishop Stanisław Dziwisz, with Cardinal Marian Jaworski, Archbishop Stanisław Ryłko and Monsignor Mieczysław Mokrzycki as concelebrants. He died at 9.37 pm—receiving the Eucharist had been his last conscious action.

Notes

1   John Paul II, *Ecclesia de Eucharistia* (2003), 8.
2   *Ibid.*
3   John Paul II, *Dominicae Cenae* (1980), 6.
4   John Paul II *Letter to the Bishop of Liege* (28 May1996).
5   John Paul II, *Dominicae Cenae*, 6.
6   John Paul II, *Letter to Children* (1994).

CONCLUSION

BY THEIR FRUITS ...

As the rain and the snow come down
from the heavens and do not return
till they have watered the earth
making it yield seed for the sower
and food for others to eat,
so is my word that goes forth out of my mouth:
it will not return to me idle
but it shall accomplish my will
the purpose for which it has been sent.

(Is 55: 6-11)

NY SPIRITUAL LIFE which does not produce concrete fruits is ultimately sterile and turned in on itself. Faith, the mustard seed, must grow, producing a harvest of good in the lives of others. As the letter of James has it: 'Faith without works is dead' (Jm 2:26) because it reveals an unconverted and spiritually dead heart.

What were the fruits of Karol Wojtyła's life and have they outlasted him?

A priest's first duty is to administer the sacraments and serve the people, materially and spiritually. He must always be prepared to speak out against injustice and at the same time be an evangeliser, bringing people into the Kingdom of Heaven and encouraging them in the quest for holiness. From his first parish in Niegowić to his appearance at the window overlooking the vast crowds, waving an olive branch and unable to speak, Wojtyła was an exemplary priest. As a teacher he was accessible to students, always available to discuss any subject they chose. As a bishop he increased vocations in his diocese and as a Pope his World Youth Days brought many conversions and vocations, helping to stem the decline that had begun in the late 1960s.

Most great councils have suffered from a turbulent aftermath, and the years after the Second Vatican Council were difficult for the Church with thousands of priests leaving the ministry. It became popular to promote the idea that a Christian could re-invent the Church's teaching according to current secular thinking or personal whim. This situation needed a clear, inspiring, and decisive voice giving the Church's authentic teaching with love and with conviction. With his encyclicals, letters and the 1992 *Catechism of the Catholic Church* John Paul II achieved this, and laid out a manifesto for the Church's future. How universally this will be heeded is not yet clear but there are signs of hope especially among the young. Certainly the Church's prophetic voice has been able to speak clearly again with the weight and testimony of tradition transmitted most recently through the documents of the Council which Pope John Paul's successor Pope Benedict XVI believed have not yet been fully absorbed.

What of John Paul's role in the great events of the last two decades of the twentieth century? It is argued that Communism as a system was always bound to fail, but the Pontificate of John Paul II undoubtedly helped to bring it down earlier than could have been predicted. Historians will no doubt cite the visits to Poland and the support for the Solidarity movement which might have been prematurely destroyed had not the world been watching. With a Pole on the chair of Peter drawing attention to the plight of his homeland, it was difficult for the Soviets to apply their usual brutality. The kidnap and murder of the young priest Jerzy Popiełuszko, which would have seemed commonplace before 1978, was a Communist blunder which increased the world's outrage.

Yet Wojtyła seldom confronted the authorities head-on. His tactic of caution had been mistaken for weakness, but it was never wise to under-rate Wojtyła. When one of his priests was arrested and imprisoned for not paying the exorbitant taxes that had been suddenly demanded of him, Bishop Wojtyła immediately replaced him as parish priest, explaining to the vast crowd why. Within a few days the priest was released and life went on as usual.[1]

When writing his biography shortly after the election of Pope John Paul II, George Blazynski interviewed many people for their opinion of the new Pope. A veteran writer and broadcaster, he was astonished to find almost no one 'from rogues to honest men' who could think of anything particularly negative to say. In the end all he could come up with were accusations that Wojtyła's sermons were too long, his written Polish often too dense and involved, and he could be impatient.[2]

As we have seen, it is impossible to discuss Karol Wojtyła in any intelligible way without reference to his intense prayer life. Long before he became Pope he possessed a quality which caused people to behave differently around him. An old friend said:

> He was the sort of person that one had to take seriously. I was never embarrassed in his presence yet he radiated a certain charisma which

stopped one behaving in a way one might well
have adopted in the presence of others. For
example, risqué jokes would be avoided in his
presence.[3]

In the film *As Good as it Gets,* Jack Nicholson is asked
for a compliment by a young woman whom he loves
but keeps offending, he thinks hard and replies 'You
make me want to be a better person'; perhaps the best
compliment that anyone can give. This was the effect
that Wojtyła, as man, priest and Pope, inspired among
those around him.

Monsignor (now Archbishop) Konrad Krajewski,
former Papal Master of Ceremonies described what it
was like to work alongside the Pope:

> He was a person filled with God. And for the
> world he had become a visible sign of an
> invisible reality, in spite of his body—disfig-
> ured by the suffering of his last years.
>
> It often sufficed just to look at him to discover
> God's presence and thus to begin to pray. This
> was enough to make one go to Confession: not
> only for one's own sins, but also for not being
> as holy as he.
>
> When he stopped being able to walk and during
> celebrations became totally dependent on the
> Masters of Ceremonies, I began to realize that
> I was touching a holy person. Perhaps I irritated
> the Vatican confessors when, before every
> celebration, I went to make my confession,
> impelled by an inner imperative and feeling a
> strong need. I needed to receive absolution in
> order to stand beside him.[4]

It is often said that no man is a hero to his valet, his wife or those close to him, yet in conversation with the authors of this book, Cardinal Dziwisz, former personal secretary to John Paul II, ended his interview by switching to English as he was leaving: 'He was a saint!' he declared.

What of the supernatural events associated with John Paul II? Not only the conversions, miraculous in themselves, but the inexplicable healings? Postulator for the late Pope's Cause, Mgr Sławomir Oder has said that unlike most canonisation causes, the cause for John Paul II was not lacking in reported miracles. In fact, in the days and weeks after John Paul's death, these seemed like an avalanche as people prayed for his intercession.

Christ warned us 'By their fruits you will know them' (Mt 7:16 and 20). For a Church that thinks in centuries, John Paul II's death is still very recent and it will take a much longer time before all the fruits are fully discerned and appreciated. The Pope who led the Church into the third Millennium is still with us and still exercising his fatherly care.

Notes

[1] G. Blazynski, *Pope John Paul: A Man from Krakow* (London: Sphere Books, 1979), p. 162.

[2] *Ibid.*, p. 176.

[3] *Ibid.*, p. 163.

[4] *L'Osservatore Romano*, English edition (11 April 2011).

APPENDIX

Prayers that John Paul II loved, and prayers written by him

The Litany of Jesus Christ, Priest and Victim
(for private use)

This litany was said each day by seminarians in Cardinal Sapieha's secret seminary in Krakow during World War II, and it remained a favourite of Pope John Paul II.

Lord have mercy
Christ have mercy.
Lord have mercy.
Christ, hear us.
Christ, graciously hear us.

God the Father of Heaven, *Have mercy on us*
God the Son, Redeemer of the world, *Have mercy on us*
God the Holy Spirit, *Have mercy on us*
Holy Trinity, one God, *Have mercy on us*
Jesus, priest and victim, *Have mercy on us*
Jesus, priest forever according to the order of Melchizedek, *Have mercy on us*
Jesus, priest whom God sent to evangelize the poor, *Have mercy on us*

Jesus, priest who at the Last Supper instituted the everlasting Sacrifice, *Have mercy on us*

Jesus, priest always living to intercede for us, *Have mercy on us*

Jesus, High Priest anointed by the Father with the Holy Spirit and with power, *Have mercy on us*

Jesus, High Priest taken from among men, *Have mercy on us*

Jesus, High Priest appointed on behalf of men, *Have mercy on us*

Jesus, High Priest of our confession of faith, *Have mercy on us*

Jesus, High Priest of a greater glory than Moses, *Have mercy on us*

Jesus, High Priest of the true Tabernacle, *Have mercy on us*

Jesus, High Priest of the good things to come, *Have mercy on us*

Jesus, High Priest, holy, innocent and undefiled, *Have mercy on us*

Jesus, High Priest, faithful and merciful, *Have mercy on us*

Jesus, High Priest of God and on fire with zeal for souls, *Have mercy on us*

Jesus, High Priest, perfect forever, *Have mercy on us*

Jesus, High Priest, who passed through the Heavens with Your own Blood, *Have mercy on us*

Jesus, High Priest, who gave eternal life for us,
Have mercy on us
Jesus, High Priest, who loved us and washed us from
our sins in Your Blood,
Have mercy on us
Jesus, High Priest, you offered *yourself* as an oblation
and victim to God,
Have mercy on us
Jesus, victim of God and of men, *Have mercy on us*
Jesus, victim, holy and immaculate,
Have mercy on us
Jesus, appeasing victim, *Have mercy on us*
Jesus, peace-making victim, *Have mercy on us*
Jesus, victim of propitiation and of praise,
Have mercy on us
Jesus, victim of reconciliation and of peace,
Have mercy on us
Jesus, victim in whom we have confidence and access
to God,
Have mercy on us
Jesus, victim living for ever and ever,
Have mercy on us

Be merciful! *Spare us, O Jesus*
Be merciful! *Graciously hear us, O Jesus*
By your eternal priesthood, *deliver us, O Jesus*
By your holy anointing, you were constituted Priest
by God the Father, *deliver us, O Jesus*
By your priestly spirit, *deliver us, O Jesus*

By your ministry, through which you have glorified your Father upon earth, *deliver us, O Jesus*
By your immolation of your precious Blood made once upon the Cross, *deliver us, O Jesus*
By your same Sacrifice renewed daily upon the altar, *deliver us, O Jesus*
By your Divine power, which you invisibly exercise in your priests, *deliver us, O Jesus*

Graciously preserve the entire priestly order in holiness of life,*We beseech you, hear us*
Graciously provide for your people pastors after your own heart, *We beseech you, hear us*
Graciously fill them with the spirit of your priesthood, *We beseech you, hear us*
Graciously grant that the lips of priests may hold knowledge, *We beseech you, hear us*
Graciously send faithful labourers into your harvest, *We beseech you, hear us*
Graciously multiply faithful stewards of your mysteries, *We beseech you, hear us*
Graciously grant them persevering service in accordance with your will, *We beseech you, hear us*
Graciously grant them meekness in the ministry, skill in action and constancy in prayer,
We beseech you, hear us
Graciously promote through them everywhere the worship of the Blessed Sacrament,
We beseech you, hear us

Graciously receive into your joy those who have
served you well, *We beseech you, hear us*

Lamb of God, you take away the sins of the world,
R. Spare us, O Lord
Lamb of God, you take away the sins of the world,
R. Graciously hear us, O Lord
Lamb of God, you take away the sins of the world,
R. Have mercy on us, O Lord

Jesus our Priest, R. Hear us
Jesus our Priest, R. Graciously hear us

O God, sanctifier and guardian of your Church,
raise up in her by your Spirit
worthy and faithful stewards of the sacred mysteries,
that by their ministry and example
the Christian people may be guided
along the way of salvation under your protection
We ask this through Christ Our Lord.
Amen.

Prayer to the Holy Spirit
(say Our Father, Hail Mary after each petition)

This prayer was given to the young Karol Wojtyła by his father and he said it daily for the rest of his life. He also recommended it to others.

Holy Spirit I ask you:

For the gift of Wisdom,
for a better understanding of you and your divine perfection.

For the gift of Understanding,
to discern clearly the spirit of the mysteries of the holy Faith.

For the gift of Counsel,
that I may live according to the principles of this Faith.

For the gift of Knowledge,
that I may look to you for help and that I may always find it in you.

For the gift of Fortitude,
that no fear or earthly preoccupations would ever separate me from you.

For the gift of Piety,
that I may always serve your majesty with a filial love.

For the gift of Fear of the Lord,
that I may dread sin which offends you O my God.

For Every Family on Earth

Lord, from you every family in Heaven and on earth takes its name . Father, you are Love and Life through your Son, Jesus Christ, born of woman and through the Holy Spirit, the fountain of divine charity. Grant that every family on earth may become for each successive generation a true shrine of life and love.

Grant that your grace may guide the thoughts and actions of husbands and wives for the good of their families and of all the families of the world.

Grant that the young may find in the family solid support for their human dignity and for their growth in truth and love.

Grant that love, strengthened by the grace of the sacrament of marriage, may prove mightier than all the weaknesses and trials through which our families sometimes pass.

Through the intercession of the Holy Family of Nazareth, grant that the Church may fruitfully carry out her worldwide mission in the family and through the family.

We ask this of you who are Life, Truth and Love, with the Son and the Holy Spirit. Amen.

Marian Prayer for Life

O Mary,
bright dawn of the new world,
Mother of the living,
to you do we entrust the cause of life:
Look down, O Mother,
upon the vast numbers
of babies not allowed to be born,
of the poor whose lives are made difficult,
of men and women
who are victims of brutal violence,
of the elderly and the sick killed
by indifference or out of misguided mercy
Grant that all who believe in your Son
may proclaim the Gospel of life
with honesty and love
to the people of our time.
Obtain for them the grace
to accept that Gospel
as a gift ever new,
the joy of celebrating it with gratitude
throughout their lives
and the courage to bear witness to it resolutely, in
order to build,
together with all people of good will,
the civilization of truth and love,
to the praise and glory of God,
the Creator and lover of life. Amen.

BIBLIOGRAPHY

John Paul II, *The Place Within—the poetry of Pope John Paul II* (London: Hutchinson, 1982)

John Paul II, *Crossing the Threshold of Hope* (London: Jonathan Cape, 1994)

John Paul II, *The Way of Prayer* (New York: Crossroads 1995)

John Paul II, *Gift and Mystery: on the 50th Anniversary of my Ordination* (New York: Image/Doubleday, 1996)

John Paul II, *Rise, Let Us Be On Our Way* (New York: Warner Books, 2004)

John Paul II, *Memory and Identity* (New York: Rizzoli, 2005)

Karol Wojtyła, (John Paul II) *Love and Responsibility* (London: Collins, 1981)

Renzo Allegri, *John Paul II, a Life of Grace* (Kindle edition, 2011)

Andrew Apostoli, *Fatima for Today: The Urgent Marian Message of Hope* (San Francisco: Ignatius Press, 2010)

George Blazynski, *Pope John Paul II: A Man from Krakow* (London: Sphere Books, 1979)

Rocco Buttiglione, *Karol Wojtyła: The Thought of the man who became Pope John Paul II* (Grand Rapids: Eerdmans, 1997)

Catechism of the Catholic Church (London: Geoffrey Chapman 1994)

Waldemar Chrostowski, *The Suffering, Closeness and Mission of the Polish Nation,* essay online at: www.georgefox.edu

Stanisław Dziwisz, *A Life with Karol* (New York: Doubleday, 2008)

Marc Foley (ed), *John of the Cross, the Ascent to Joy* (New York: New City Press, 2002)

André Frossard, *Be Not Afraid! André Frossard in conversation with John Paul II* (London: Bodley Head, 1984)

James Hitchcock, *History of the Catholic Church* (San Francisco: Ignatius Press, 2012)

John of the Cross, *Collected Works* (Washington DC: Institute of Carmelite Studies, 1991)

Jerzy Kluger, *The Pope and I* (New York: Orbis Books, 2012)

Maria Faustina Kowalska, *Diary: Divine Mercy in my Soul* (Stockbridge, USA: Marian Press, 2011)

Brendan Leahy, *Believe in Love: The Life, Ministry and Teachings of John Paul II* (Dublin: Veritas, 2011)

Mieczyslaw Malinksi, *Pope John Paul II: The Life of My Friend Karol Wojtyla.* (London: Burns and Oates, 1979)

Mieczyslaw Mokrzycki with Brygida Grysiak, *He Liked Tuesdays Best: A Story about Everyday Life of the Blessed John Paul* (Krakow: Wydawnictwo publishing, 2011)

Garry O'Connor, *Universal Father, a Life of John Paul II* (London: Bloomsbury Publishing, 2006)

William Oddie (ed). *John Paul the Great* (London: Catholic Truth Society, 2003)

Slawomir Oder with Saverio Gaeta, *Why he is a Saint: the Life and Faith of Pope John Paul II and the Cause for Canonisation* (USA: Rizzoli International, 2010)

Emily Stimpson, *These Beautiful Bones: An Everyday Theology of the Body* (Steubenville USA: Emmaus Road Publishing, 2013)

Tad Szulc, *Pope John Paul II, The Biography* (New York: Simon and Schuster, 1995)

Teresa of Avila, trans. J Cohen, *Autobiography* (London: Penguin Classics, 1987)

Timothy Tindal-Robertson, *Fatima, Russia, and Pope John Paul II* (Leominster: Gracewing, 1992)

George Weigel, *Witness to Hope: The Biography of Pope John Paul II* (New York and London: HarperCollins, 1999)

George Weigel, *The End and the Beginning: Pope John Paul II — the Victory of Freedom, the Last Years, the Legacy* (New York and London: Doubleday, 2010)

Christopher West, *At the Heart of the Gospel: Reclaiming the Body for the New Evangelisation* (New York: Image Books, 2012)

Cecilia Wolkowinska, with Joanna Bogle, *When the Summer Ended* (Leominster: Gracewing Publishing, 1992)

Lino Zani, *The Secret Life of John Paul II* (USA: St Benedict Press, 2012)

Pawel Zuchniewicz, *Miracles of John Paul II* (Toronto: Catholic Youth Studio, 2006)

Lightning Source UK Ltd.
Milton Keynes UK
UKOW04f1807270817
308025UK00002B/67/P